Jemimah Adewunmi

Young**Writers** 2005 POETRY COMPETITION

PLayground Poets

Let your creativity flow...

D1744639

ode

limerick   haiku

rhyme

Balle

London
Edited by Steve Twelvetree

 Young**Writers**

First published in Great Britain in 2005 by:
Young Writers
Remus House
Coltsfoot Drive
Peterborough
PE2 9JX
Telephone: 01733 890066
Website: www.youngwriters.co.uk

SB ISBN 1 84602 147 2

Foreword

Young Writers was established in 1991 and has been passionately devoted to the promotion of reading and writing in children and young adults ever since. The quest continues today. Young Writers remains as committed to the fostering of burgeoning poetic and literary talent as ever.

This year's Young Writers competition has proven as vibrant and dynamic as ever and we are delighted to present a showcase of the best poetry from across the UK. Each poem has been carefully selected from a wealth of *Playground Poets* entries before ultimately being published in this, our thirteenth primary school poetry series.

Once again, we have been supremely impressed by the overall high quality of the entries we have received. The imagination, energy and creativity which has gone into each young writer's entry made choosing the best poems a challenging and often difficult but ultimately hugely rewarding task - the general high standard of the work submitted amply vindicating this opportunity to bring their poetry to a larger appreciative audience.

We sincerely hope you are pleased with our final selection and that you will enjoy *Playground Poets London* for many years to come.

Contents

Abercorn School

Rianna Hendricks (7)	60
Waneta Newell (10)	61
Iman Benazha (7)	61
Zion Chetram (9)	62
Siane Ashanti (7)	62
Rochelle McLeod (8)	63
Nathan Rhoden (10)	63
Mohamed Idris (10)	64
Paula Tudek (10)	64
Annabelle Lognon (7)	65
Yasmine Benazha (9)	65
Akilah Barnabie (9)	66
Shana Chanel Osbourne (8)	66
Jamell Christie (9)	67
Dana Barnett (6)	67
Gianina Graham (9)	68
Tianna Charles (8)	68
Nakira Phillips (9)	69
Rianne Wright (8)	69
Rike Adeniran (9)	70
Jadesayo Adelekan (9)	70
Anjelah Kugendra (7)	71
Oyinkansola Otukoya (9)	71
Domonique Smith (11)	72
Isaac Kizza (8)	72
Cassandra Parkes (11)	73
Shamaree Wilson (9)	73
Haider Bashir (10)	74
Venezia Justinne Pitter (10)	74
Chika Njoku (10)	75
Bianca Courtney (11)	75
Zainab Jalloh (10)	76
Selina Dyer (9)	76
Ebyan Abdirahman (10)	77
Matthew Kayembe (6)	77
Andrea Feyisayo-Odedina (10)	78
Oyabola Oyesoro (10)	78
Don Brown (9)	79
Rania Saeed (7)	79
Tanya Sheree Stern (8)	80
Taiye Fashipe (10)	80
Miles Lindsay (10)	81

Brenda Mshiu (8)   81
Hanaa Bashir (7)   82
Joshua Parkes (8)   82
Shemond Dale (9)   83
Benjamin Currie (9)   83
Rowan Edwards (9)   84
Cherelle Thompson (11)   84
Reion Tibby (10)   85
Aimen Idris (8)   85
Mathun Kuganesan (6)   86
Patrice King (10)   86
Zahra Ahmedali (5)   86
Isobel Rose Adedeji (6)   87
Savannah-Rae Judith Wright (10)   87
Layla Bradford (6)   88
Jordan Raeburn (10)   89
Abigail Abena Gyesi (10)   90
Deborah Orukotan (7)   91
Tyana Lynch (7)   91
Louise Jesi (7)   92
Siobhan Mitchell (7)   92
Sassikia Jarrett (6)   93
Daniel Otukoya (6)   93
Jamal Liam Brown (10)   94
Dion Rene Upton (7)   94
Kanyin Fagade (11)   95
Raphael Louis (11)   95

Mitchell Brook Primary School
Nicole Charles (8)   96
Zhane Finikin (8)   96
Halima Akinyemi (8)   97
Ayodele Narh (8)   98
Talika Pathiranage (9)   99

Princess Frederica School
Katinka Achrafie (9)   99
Tom Pomphrey (11)   100
Ruth Bertulis-Fernandes (11)   101
Daniel Eugene (11)   102
Eya Taylor (6)   102

Shahid Miah (11)   118
Jahid Miah (7)   119
Nieka Payne (8)   119
Ruby Arscott (8)   120
Lucy Allen (10)   120
Jéan-Paul Rama (8)   120
Zainab Olaoye (7)   121
Luka Kenyon (8)   121
Clemmie Kenyon (8)   121
Krishen Patten (10)   122
David Gyamfi (8)   122
Olivia Santoro (7)   123
Bethan Powell (8)   123
Joel Bennett (10)   124
Samira Haque (7)   124
Laurence Balfour (7)   124
Aeron Holland-Lewis (8)   125
Portia Baker (11)   125
Roisin Ellis (7)   126
Rose Leach (7)   126
Benjamin Allen (7)   127
Keenan Trotman Guy (10)   127
Elliot Whitely (10)   127
Renece Harrison (11)   128
Jade Licorish (10)   128
Rhiannon Whitely (10)   128

St Mary's RC Primary School, Kilburn
Annie Clarke (9)   129
David Twumasi (10)   129
Jessica Assaad (11)   130
Grace Horan (11)   130
Nicole Mendes (10)   131
Chloe Wilkins (10)   131
Connor Spaans (10)   132
Taijarne Scott-Chandler (10)   132
Decio De Freitas (10)   133
Ryan Jinadu (11)   133
Gabriel Solomon (9)   134
Sharon Ihemesinwa (10)   134
Cameron Vaz (9)   135

The Hampshire School

West Green JMI School

Lucas Trattou (10)	155
Daniel Harris (11)	156
Radha Wahyuwidayat (8)	157
Esra Mansour	158

Westminster Cathedral Choir School

Edward Hacking (9)	159
James Machin (9)	159
Lawrence Speaight (8)	160
Philippe Marchant (9)	160
Jasper Ford-Welman (9)	160
Christopher Short (8)	161
Alasdair Grassie (9)	161
Ferdinand Rex (8)	162
Oliver Swan (9)	162
George Mitchell (9)	163
Oliver Togias-Howells (8)	163
Nicholas Eterovic (8)	164
Theo Bakker (8)	164
Julian Hartley (8)	165
Luke Olver (8)	165
Barnaby Lynch (8)	166
Roland Abbott (8)	166
Charles Ingell (8)	166
Edward Hackett (8)	167
Charlie Davies (8)	167
Peter Burke-Smith (8)	168

Whitmore Primary School

Kamil Sekerali (10)	168
Nathifa Dawkins-Alexander (11)	169
Tyrelle Glasgow (11)	169
Alex Demetriou (8)	169
Dami Jinadu (10)	170
Precious Omorogbe (8)	170
Mehmet Gerekli (9)	171
Anh Pham (9)	171
Jay Fenton (8)	171
Nicole Ansell (10)	172
Kaya Fedai (9)	172

Tashana Destouche (8)	172
Flore Kadianga (10)	173
Farren Cummings (10)	173
Sevgi Firat (9)	173
Kevin Voang (9)	174
Shae Oram (8)	174
Dina Sammut (9)	174
Anna Oluwalana (8)	175

Wyvil Primary School

Anthony Mba (9)	175
Gustavo Hondrato (10)	176
Segun Soji-Akingboye (10)	176
Adaeze Ugochukwu (9)	177
Latifaha Ireland (10)	177
Emmanuel Oguntimirin (10)	178
Le-Reisse Douglas (10)	179
Sofia Cabral (10)	179
Abigail Ashmead (9)	180
Alfredtina Boaitey (10)	180
Nicole Stephenson (10)	181
Tasharn Simms (9)	181
Asia Vassel (9)	182
Rianna Stroude (9) & Suzie Alves (10)	182
Yasmine Gittens-Sextius (9)	183
Deji Adegboyega (8)	184
Natasha Oviri (10)	184
Jermaine Elor (9)	185
Rasak Obanigba (10)	185
Qurratuaina Awangkechik (8)	186
Marcio Andrade (9)	186

The Poems

The Short And Sad Life Of Maude Atkinson

In a house off Downshire Lane
Lived a peaceful family of three
A girl of six looked out of the window
She said, 'I want to climb that tree!'

'Come now, Maude, that's too high!'
Said her mum who was very nice
But Maude, you know, she didn't give up
And whined and whinged so much suffice.

They ate their dinner in silence
For Maude had ceased to grumble
I'll do it tonight! she thought
As she ate her apple crumble.

While everyone slept in their homes
Maude sprinted towards that tree
She ran towards that destination
Screaming, 'That's the tree for me!'

She jumped up to the first branch
Which, because of winter, was bare
Growing more and more excited
She climbed as fast as a hare!

Then a crack – and a scream cried out
Followed by a thump on the ground
The screeches were amazing
The sounds were heard all around.

'Ashes to ashes, dust to dust
Let Maude rest in peace.'
Everyone was silent;
The weeping did not cease.

Natalia Green (10)
Abercorn School

Brain Surgery

So my mum took me to the most
Boring place ever
She thought I just had
A cold or a fever.

But just in case this
Meant extreme pain
She took me to the place
For surgery for the brain.

He cut my head open
But there was nothing inside
Brain-cells on vacation
With a lousy tour guide.

What a lovely sight
To see for a cell
So the doctor suggested,
'Here's a pea, for your head, guard it well.'

So my friends called me pea brain
For them it was fun
But just past my lunchtime
My pea brain was gone!

Sean Connor (10)
Abercorn School

The Horse

Who let them loose with the peanut butter?
Who gave them a smooth coat?
Who made them look like a big reindeer?
Who made them run like the wind?
Who designed them big and strong?
Who painted them brown and white?
Who thought to give them a big hairy mane
For each newborn foal?

Agnes Storen (9)
Abercorn School

Sports

They keep you busy every day,
Sports are really fun to play!
If it's netball, swimming, golf or football,
Cricket, tennis, bikes or baseball,
All of them are filled with fun –
The type of fun for everyone!

They make you really fit and strong,
They keep you healthy all day long,
Occasionally you might get hurt
Or fall off your bike into the dirt,
But who would care – they got a scratch
While playing an exciting cricket match?

So next time you've finished your homework,
And you're sticking to the television like glue,
Go outside and bring a ball
- you know what you should do.

Shivani Oberoi (10)
Abercorn School

Nature's Beauty

Nature has a beauty,
Reflected in your eyes,
The trees in the ground,
And the apples for gooseberry pies.

Nature is so passionate
It could almost make me faint,
The birds so small, the giraffes so tall,
And the baby seals sticking their noses in a pot of paint!

Nature has so many colours and flowers,
It's really hard to choose,
But I like the roses red and the violets blue,
Even though they're not as sweet as you.

Zoe Silkstone (9)
Abercorn School

Evil

Great wisdom lies within,
The greatest lords of fantasy.
But even lords so intelligent
Cannot stand up to evil
And when evil invades the mind,
There is no escape.

Only some lords,
Are born with the power to destroy,
But still . . .
. . . they never live to see the world,
Shining and happy,
Filled with joy
And freed from evil.

If you live,
To see evil destroyed,
You should know that evil,
Never sleeps.

Egmontas Gerasimovas (10)
Abercorn School

How I Make Tea

First I put water into my kettle,
I look at my brother doing skateboard tricks,
Now the water has had time to settle,
I turn the cooker on number six.

I put the kettle on and wait,
And when it screams out in pain,
Ready to pour – there's no time to debate,
Oh dear, it looks like it is going to rain!

In comes my brother all soggy and wet,
And sits at the table with nothing to say,
I know what he wants and I quickly get,
The teapot and cups with a bag of Earl Grey.

Daniel Vukelich (10)
Abercorn School

Light And Dark

When the sun rises
With the bloom of its light,
There is no crisis,
Just the spirit of right.

When it goes down,
In the dusky dawn,
The Earth will be covered,
With a big black storm.

When the moon rises,
It lights the sky once again,
There are no surprises,
Just the spirits remain.

For the light and the dark,
It is no trick,
It will rise on its mark
And go down with a flick.

Alice Haguenauer (10)
Abercorn School

Rainy Days

Pitter-patter, pitter-patter
Down comes the rain
Hitting on the leaves of the trees
Falling down on the grass so green.

Sliding on the soaking grass
As my shirt stains green
And feel the rain on my knee
And the rain soaking me like I'm in a pool.

Pitter-patter, pitter-patter
The rain comes down faster, I head for the door
As I head for the door
I see the rain come down and pour.

Andy Bohl (9)
Abercorn School

Beauty And The Feast

This boring old story's had its share of glory
The story of Beauty and the Beast
It's boring and dull, more dull than so dull
So I changed it to Beauty and the feast.

Well you see, the Beauty well of course that is me
And the Beast is now all of my feast
Potatoes and chives, lemonade, Five Alive
And - well giant bread with too much yeast.

Pudding, oh pudding, how I love my pudding
Banofee pie, cake and chocolate dots
Oh no what is happening, this food is quite fattening
And my skin's breaking out into spots.

I've realised I'm no longer pure,
Oh God, I wish there was a cure
I shouldn't have eaten that feast
Mrs Teapot, Clocksworth and Lumiere said.
Which really started to hurt my head,
'You shouldn't have eaten the beast!'

Georgia Summers (11)
Abercorn School

The Forest

The forest is dark and cruel,
The trees blow the squirrels and fall.
The eagle's determined and evil face,
Waits for the great chase.
Then comes the chaos.

The enormous, tall trees,
Are covered in lots of bees.
The animals are terrified of the night,
But the moon holds some light.
The eagle wins its crown over the animals.

James Pike-Watson (10)
Abercorn School

Best Friend

I have a best friend!
I really like her
We meet everyday
And play all sorts of games.
She's my best friend,
And always will be!

My best friend is great!
I never knew a girl like her!
We sit next to each other at school
We play together at breaks.
We go everywhere together,
People say we're stuck with glue!

I love playing with my best friend.
We always play together.
Sometimes we play football,
Sometimes we play basketball.
I like running,
My best friend likes playing with balls.

I have a best friend!
I really like her!
We're always together,
'Cause we really like each other!
We'll always be best friends,
No matter what happens.

Agniete Gerasimovaite (9)
Abercorn School

Dinosaurs

Dinosaurs are fierce and scary
Some are gentle and some are wary.

Most eat meat and the others eat plants
Some are small and some are giants.

Achilles Camble (7)
Abercorn School

Would You Rather Be . . .

Would you rather be . . .
Stuck in a spiralling spaceship
Or be grounded for a month?

Would you rather be . . .
Chased by a hungry lion
Or be in a boxing ring with a fierce gorilla?

Would you rather be . . .
In a pool filled with poisonous gas
Or in a tub full of spaghetti bolognaise?

Would you rather be . . .
Running cross country in the slush
Or be in a spine-chilling horror movie?

Would you rather be . . .
In a room filled with ferocious rottweilers
Or be playing cricket in Lords cricket ground?

Jai Malhotra (9)
Abercorn School

The Senses Of Art

The glue tastes bitter when I bite it off my nail
Trays of watercolours are weak and pale.
The poster paint smells of nothing
I can hear the paintbrush brushing.

As I pick my palette up carefully
And make movements with my brush gracefully
I paint with acrylics and oils
Beautiful princesses, witches with boils.

The plaster makes the air cloudy white
Scattered bits of coloured paper make the room bright
The feel of paint gushing through your fingers
Rusty scissors cutting sounds like famous singers.

Rebecca Anthony (9)
Abercorn School

Why Does It Happen?

Why does it happen?
Mother Earth's wrath.
Why does it happen?
The sea's bubbly froth.
Why does it happen?
The Earth's violent tremble.
Why does it happen?
The volcano's eruption of fury.
Why does it happen?
The stormy waves destroying the shore.
Why does it happen?
The luminescent spinning top of the ocean.
Why does it happen?
The dusty swirl of the cone.
Why does it happen?
The intelligent creation of petrol transformed into a recipe
For disaster.
Why . . .?

Shikha Pahari (11)
Abercorn School

My Baby Brother

Everybody thinks my baby brother is so cute,
But actually:
He's fat and bald,
He looks weird and old,
And he screams in the middle of the night,
Instead of a twinkle,
He has a wrinkle,
In his bluish eyes,
His mouth is hollow,
Which means as follows:
He doesn't have any teeth!
Oh, how I wish my brother was older than me!

Gabriel Salitan-Alvarez (10)
Abercorn School

My Holiday

When I have my winter holiday,
Every time I go far away.
I went to Switzerland this year,
To the mountains near Geneva.
When I was skiing on the slope,
I was doing a snow plough,
And I had the only hope,
To come down safe somehow.
I have got a medal and some skills,
And now I am a Red League Prince.
I will try to ski much faster
And become a great ski master!

Dimitry Karavaikin (8)
Abercorn School

Music

Sweet, soft
Soaring, flowing, floating
Angels speaking in melody
Crashing, ringing, beating
Powerful, thunderous
Music.

Victoria Hoffmeister (9)
Abercorn School

In The Playground

In the playground there are swings and slides,
Why don't you come and play seek and hide?

In the playground roundabouts go round,
Swings swing and make a funny sound.

In the playground, I climb on the climbing frames,
Or play a good game of Princes and Dames.

Jessica Bill (7)
Abercorn School

The Pet

When I woke up,
I ran to a vet,
I thought I was on time,
And I was scared,
But it was too late,
I made a mistake,
And it happened,
I lost my pet,
Everybody had faith,
Except one,
The vet.
He thought he did a good job,
But not,
And the pet was gone,
For ever.

Robert Pflaumer (10)
Abercorn School

What Car Will I Have?

What car will I have when I grow up?
Will I have a Mercedes?
What car will I have?

Will I have a Porsche,
A BMW, Golf or Volkswagen,
Beetle, Volvo or Polo,
Citroen, Smart or Ford?
They are all cars.

Maybe big cars:
Jeep, Range Rover or Landrover,
Or those for the countryside.

Or very fast
Ferrari, Lamborghini or McLaren?

Raffi Haguenauer (8)
Abercorn School

Tsunami

Tranquil, peaceful, evening
Sea
Happy, noisy, celebrating
People
Tired, weary, sleepy
People
Slumbering, contented, unaware
People
Tranquil, peaceful, morning
Sea
Violent, powerful, angry
Sea
Petrified, running, despairing, panicking, courageous, parting
People
Drowning, rag-doll, silent
People
Tranquil, peaceful, morning
Sea.

Emma Hulme (11)
Abercorn School

A Book

If all the books were piled together, how high would they be?
Up to the moon or up to the stars, it simply entrances me.
Robert Muchamore can amaze me no more
Anthony Horowitz too.
Books for everyone
Books for all
My love for books will never fall.

Books about justice
Books about feud
Books can enhance anyone's mood.

Angus Smith (10)
Abercorn School

Dreams

Dreams, wonderful, exciting, full of surprises!
Seeping into you,
Filling you with sorrow and happiness.
Bringing light to your world,
Letting your imagination run free.
Giving you perfect serenity.
Making you feel beautiful and carefree.
Healing pain and stress,
Sometimes this is all we need,
Dreams.

Phoebe Norton (11)
Abercorn School

Hairy Fairy

There was a fairy
Who was hairy,
And a cat
Who had a hat,
A dog that could
Change into a frog,
And a fairy
That was wary.

Harry Pourdjis (8)
Abercorn School

Lion

Lion oh lion,
How fast and speedy.

Lion oh lion,
How bold and greedy.

Lion oh lion,
How frightful and scary!

Oliver Pattni (7)
Abercorn School

The Relatives

My mum is always glum
My dad is always sad
My sister's always got a blister
My brother is always in a bother
My mouse is always in its house
My gran has to ban me from her house
My cousin is a young one
My chum has a big tum
The cat is fat!

But I love them all because they're family!

Lucy Streeten (8)
Abercorn School

When I Grow Up I Want To Be . . .

When I grow up I want to be
A vet, so I can pet various animals.

When I grow up I want to be
An artist so I can paint saints.

When I grow up I want to be
A computer whiz
So I can teach children like Doris,
Anne and Liz.

Shrishti Menon (8)
Abercorn School

My Family And Me

There lived my family and me!
My brother had a dog called Flea.
My sister had a cat called Lee.
My mother had a parrot called Dee.
I had a baby brother called G.
And all he could say was 'mee.'

Onose Egualeonan (7)
Abercorn School

You're An Angel Now!

Grandma you're an angel now
Floating on a cloud,
You brought happiness to this Earth
And made your family proud,
Nothing could replace you
Or your beautiful smile,
At least you're with the angels
Where you truly do fit in,
Every grandparent is special
In their family's eyes,
But you were an angel
Sent down in disguise,
And I'm so sad to know that
Your time with us is gone,
It's time for you to disappear
Back up where you belong,
Sleep sweet angel
Peaceful on a cloud,
I'm looking for your glowing star
Stand out and make us proud!

Rest in peace I love you sweet Grandma
    Love Darius.

Idemudia Egualeoran (10)
Abercorn School

Weather

February, frosty fogs,
Winter shivers, fire-warmed logs.

July joy means school is out,
Sandy castles, friends to stay.

December's dark, full of light,
Christmas carols, stars so bright.

Eleanor Thwaites (8)
Abercorn School

What Would It Be Like?

What would it be like
To ride a sleek silver wolf in the night,
And never stop or get off?

What would it be like
To swim with dolphins in the freshwater sea
In the morning,
When it's never too shallow?

What would it be like
To have a room full of animals,
Big ones and small ones,
Live ones and cuddly ones?

Jack Harvey (10)
Abercorn School

An Alligator

Who let them loose with a scaly tail
And gave them razor teeth?
Who made them look like a green platform?
Who made them so fearsome?
Who designed them so big and greedy?
Who painted them all green?
Who thought to give them lumpy skin
For each newborn baby alligator?

Alex Pabarcius (8)
Abercorn School

My Pet

My pet is a goldfish
My pet goldfish is called Goldy.
Goldy doesn't eat a lot
But I think Goldy is all full up.
I wish Goldy was a girl!

Aiko Miyamato (8)
Abercorn School

Friends

Friends are great,
They're always there for you,
They're nice, kind, loving, gentle,
Bold and brave too.
They always try to help you
In every sort of way.
Sometimes when I hurt them,
I just don't see it in every way.
I must get better at this, and my friends
Are by my side,
I love them as much as the stars above
And I can't bear to lose them.
I really love them, I really, really, really love them.
I love my friends,
Please be my friend.

Letitia O'Neill (8)
Abercorn School

My Dad And Mum

My dad is tall
He is not small
My dad is kind
I watch TV he never does mind
He is very helpful
He never falls
I am so glad that he is my dad.

Mum is small
She is not tall
She helps me do my homework
I help her to do her work
My mum is nice
She hates mice
I love my mum and that is all.

Isabella Potes (8)
Abercorn School

My Future

When I grow up
Will there still be
Food and water?

Will there be
Wars or peace
And anymore killing?

Will there be
Trees and forests
With any plants and animals left?

Will there be
Pure water left to drink?
Will the sea still be blue?

Will there be
Anymore pollution?
Will anything still be clean?

Will there be
Anymore natural disasters
Like earthquakes, tsunamis and volcanic eruptions?

After all that
What will be left?
Anything on Earth?

Jek Woo (9)
Abercorn School

Wind

The wind blew me to school today in a funny sort of way.
It took me through a bench, down the drain,
Through the park and back again.
The wind blew me to school
Wouldn't it be cool if the wind blew you to school?

Francesca Dacosta (8)
Abercorn School

In The Park

Down in the park I met a girl called Vicky.
Vicky said, 'I can't play now, this honey is so sticky.'

Down in the park I met a girl called Floa.
Floa said, 'I can't play now
I can't find my brother Yo.'

Down in the park I met a girl called Grace.
Grace said, 'I can't play now
I've got to go to the palace.'

Madeleine Gledhill (8)
Abercorn School

The Giraffe

Who let them loose with peanut butter and lemons?
Who gave them necks as long as snakes?
Who made them look like trees?
Who made them have legs as long as a road?
Who designed them with such small ears?
Who painted them yellow with brown dots?
Who thought to give them long tails with a blob
For each newborn giraffe?

Aatikah Mouti (8)
Abercorn School

Bat

Who let them loose with the black paint?
Who gave them sharp fangs?
Who made them look like the night sky?
Who made then nocturnal?
Who designed them to suck blood?
Who painted them black and sinister?
Who thought to give them black jackets
For each newborn baby bat?

Rayan Asfari (9)
Abercorn School

Playing With Fire

Fire was born from one match
From a little short spark
Then it jumped to the candle
It has found its place
Fire is peaceful and still
Fire is warm
Fire is grateful to me for its birth
Fire is shining
Fire is moving
Fire is playing with me and the candle
After a while the candle starts crying
Its tears are rolling beneath
The candle gets smaller
The candle gets weaker
And slowly loses its height
Fire is burning
Fire is angry
Fire is sharp and sharper its flame
It has an evil streak to it
It can jump to the table below
It can jump to the curtains above
It can glow all over your house
But my fire is playing with me and the candle
Fire can bite
But it is friendly to me
As I let it alight
It's burning and laughing and dancing with me.

Alina Filchukova (12)
Abercorn School

I Was A Goldfish

I was a goldfish swimming in the Thames,
With my family and friends; until, a man came and took me away.
Then I was trapped, in a tank
With many other fish.
Suddenly,
Ten minutes later,
A girl took me and another fish in a bag!
I saw this sort of fur-ball;
Then I was put in a bowl.
The fur-ball jumped
Onto the counter,
Scratched open the bowl,
And sadly killed my friend!
The girl came in astonishment,
And saw the disaster,
And then put me in the best place ever,
The Thames.

Christakis Constanti (9)
Abercorn School

Fruit For Pets

I had a big polar bear,
Who thought he was a pear!
And a fish,
Who thought he could wish!

I had a dog,
Who thought he lived in a bog!
And a cat,
Who thought he was a bat!

One day when I woke up,
I did a hiccup.
So I went downstairs to try to get a fright,
Well, I did because . . . my pets were right!

Zachary Hall (8)
Abercorn School

My Future

When I grow up
Will there still be
Trees and forests?

Will there be
Clean water and
Will there be animals around?

Will there be
Wars and lots of killing
Or will we have peace?

Will there be
Rubbish everywhere
Or will we recycle?

Will there be
Lots more tsunamis
Or any more tornadoes?

Will anything be
On this Earth
For me when I grow up?

Tatyana Isaac (8)
Abercorn School

My Name Is Lorcan

My name is Lorcan
I'm friends with Duncan
I play PS2
And have a dog called Fu-Fu.

I have a good profession
And live in a different dimension.
In the black hole
Near the North Pole.

Lorcan Brannigan (8)
Abercorn School

Now She Is Gone

She was bold and brave
She always made you feel safe
She was as gentle as a dove
And as fierce as a lion
She was as black as the night sky
And as white as snow
She was picky and stubborn
But never got on my nerves.

Now she is gone.

End all the stories
Close all the doors
Stop the world circling
And the sun shall burn no more.

She was psychic
But surprised at surprises
She was as quiet as a mouse
And as loud as an elephant
She was silky soft
And very prickly
I miss the way she used to curl up on my bed
I miss the way she gave you the cheek
Even though she couldn't talk
I miss her fights with the neighbours' first cat
And her friendship with the other.

Now she is gone

End all the stories
Close all the doors
Stop the world circling
And the sun shall burn no more.

Jodan Trotman (11)
Berrymede Junior School

Missing You Uncle John

Missing you Uncle John,
When I am down.
Missing you Uncle John,
Just want you around.
Don't want you to leave,
Just want you to stay here with me please.
Missing you Uncle John,
Don't forget about me.

Missing you Uncle John,
Want you here right now.
Missing you Uncle John,
When I think of you, I think *Oh Wow!*
Missing you Uncle John,
You were so helpful and kind.
Missing you Uncle John,
You had a great mind.

Missing you Uncle John,
You were working and clever.
Missing you Uncle John.
You were silly and tall.
Missing you Uncle John.

Summer Leach (10)
Berrymede Junior School

My ABC and 123

My grandma is my ABC
My 123
She makes me solid
When I am down,
She is my legs, my mouth and my heart,
Also my eyes.
If I lose my grandma,
I will lose every single one of my grandparents,
She is the only one left.
She is my healthy, wealthy, strict, funny grandma
I love her as much as a dog loving her new baby to bits.

She is my ABC,
Also my 123,
Grandma I love you to bits.
She buys me bags of clothes, the whole wardrobe sometimes,
I love my clothes,
She is like my mate.
I talk to her like an agony aunt,
She gives me very good advice,
She buys me chicken from KFC, McDonalds and loads more.
I love her too much
I will never forget her
Never!
That is why she is . . .
My ABC, my 123.

Juliet Akigg (10)
Berrymede Junior School

I Never Knew

I never knew I could miss her so much,
I never knew.
I never knew I could cry so much,
I never knew.
I never knew it would feel like this,
I never knew.
I never knew this feeling would stay,
I never knew.
I never knew I would have a hole in my heart,
I never knew.
I never knew my heart would have a piece missing,
I never knew.
I never knew my heart would tighten,
I never knew.
I never knew my eyes would never see her again,
I never knew.
I never knew.
I never knew.

Rania Jundi (11)
Berrymede Junior School

Jade

I miss Jade so much, I cry everyday,
She was my morning and evening star,
My sunshine, my rain, my world.
Jade was very loveable,
She was always there,
She was very forgiving,
I wish I were more like her.
She was funny,
And liked to joke around.
Jade loved hamsters and all furry things,
She never lied to anyone, or me,
Except the odd once or twice.

Tai Tong (10)
Berrymede Junior School

Missing My Cousin

I am missing my cousin
His name is Ajdin
He is in high school
He is sporty, his fav' is footy.

He loves budgies
He loves playing with them.

He is skinny and thirteen years old
He has brown hair
He is tall
He is trustworthy
He is caring and cool
He is strong and fast.

This is why I miss my cousin.

Elvis Belasic (11)
Berrymede Junior School

I'm Missing My Grandma A Lot

I'm missing my grandma a lot,
She was very friendly,
She was also very caring,
And very funny.

I'm missing my grandma a lot,
She had black hair,
And brown eyes,
Her skin was very fair.

I'm missing my grandma a lot,
She was my north, south, east and west,
She was my grandma,
And she was the best.

Farddin Nasrat (10)
Berrymede Junior School

I Miss Her So Much

I miss her so much.
She was really funny,
She always made me laugh.
Her ginger hair brushed into her face,
Her golden freckles stood out.
I miss her so much.
Every time she fell or started bleeding,
She never cried,
She was so brave.
I miss her so much.
She was really tall,
Very cool and girly,
She was always happy,
She was my best friend.
I miss her so much.
She was really sensitive.
When I left,
She started crying.
It was the first time I'd seen her crying.
I miss her so much.

Arazoo Kadir (11)
Berrymede Junior School

A Sailor's Pocket . . .

A telescope to keep on guard
A torn and tattered playing card,
A book to learn how to tie knots
And bits of broken lobster pots,
A golden compass showing west
A fragment from a seagull's nest,
A sharp and pointed iron hook
A small and sodden, red notebook,
Foggy, misty broken glass
A gleaming coin of finest brass.

Hilaire Blyth (8)
Falkner House

Cat

Slithering delicately over fields,
The stream seeps rapidly, avoiding the twigs that obstruct its pain,
The cat patters along the hilly landscape,
Its shadow long and slender stretched onto the dry ground.

Two eyes like deep green pools,
Scan the scene for its unlucky prey,
Claws clench, irritated at the fact
That no mice are visible in the darkness of the woods.

The woods reflect in its dark eyes,
Like mirrors with pin-prick pupils at the centre,
Craftily navigates the closest prey
Two green circles bold in the black.

Its back arches, it hears a sound
A scuttle? A scurry? A mouse?
It accelerates to a quick dart,
Preparing for the pounce.

Silence. A gust of wind twists the leaves,
The mouse is dead.
The cat slinks off with pride,
Slithering over the riverbanks, winding round the trees.

Elizabeth Peet (11)
Falkner House

The Hedgehog

No twig snaps under its fragile feet
Full-leaved trees shade a thorny back
Scrambles over: rotten logs, through dense bushes, under thorn
hedges
A hedgehog curls into a ball of spikes.

Eyes, deep pools of black
Stare wide, concentrating on the Earth
Sharp stones scattered on the dry soil
Toughen the skin on its feet.

Delicate ears prick on its small head
Absorbing the sound
Nose scavengers around the tree trunks
Prickles protruding from its body like spears.

An intruder emerges
Into the hedgehog's territory
The hedgehog shuffles, his spikes glimmering
As the stranger slinks towards him.

The hedgehog ambles
Through the sharp blades of grass
That pierce his stomach
As he flits into the dense undergrowth.

Georgia Richards (11)
Falkner House

The Lizard

Flits in and out of tiny speckled stones
Scuttles like a spider
Sliding up the palm tree on a shady branch
Coconuts sway in the wind, rattling together like castanets
Tail quivers, feet like suction pads
Tongue forked like a match flame, flickers
Plucks at hovering mosquitoes
A born gymnast
Life like a dance routine
Turning flips
Flimsy skeleton like a pencil lead, snappable
Light body; so light the wind could carry this creature
And throw it onto the shingly beach.

The lizard basks in the scorching sun
He writhes and darts down the tread bark
Tracks unnoticed
Like a gypsy, it has no home
Always on the move, exploring new places
Bold and unflinching
Escaping every trouble
Hiding under dry rocks
Smiling slyly.

Sophie Aldrich (10)
Falkner House

Mighty Marmalade

His eyes as green as emeralds
Staring at the crack
Waiting for the mice to peer
Not sleeping nor turning back.

His teeth as sharp as needles
Tearing, ripping, biting,
Eating in the blink of an eye
As fiercely as his fighting.

His whiskers twitch and quiver
Long and thin and white
Waving to and fro
Reflecting all the light.

He stalks and he prowls
He controls the place!
Patrolling all the while
Keeping watch on every shoelace.

His fur is soft as velvet
And so orange and so bright
His name is Mighty Marmalade
And he's the purr-fect cat, don't you think that's right?

Bridget Cullinan (8)
Falkner House

Lioness

Proud queen
Stealthy hunter,
Alone and alert.

Dark eyed
She searches,
Through the coarse, yellow grasses.

Golden coat
Fierce, muscular,
Making no sound.

Grass flattened
Paws padding
Shadow, hidden.

Antelope glimpsed,
Chosen and cornered
Tail coiled.

Crouching back
On strong legs,
She prepares.

Timing exact,
Pounces and attacks,
Teeth sinking into flesh.

Dominique Jones (11)
Falkner House

Snake

Perched on the roughness of the chair,
My watch ticking
In the silence of the dark
Reminding me of a snake's rattle.

The scales of the snake, dry
Dry as crackers at Christmas time,
Slithering through sand
Golden colour of skin glistening in hot days.

Flying through the sand, quick as sound,
Hissing like the first steam train
Arriving at Manchester,
The snake is sinewy, rolling up in spirals.

Like a serpent on the head of Medusa
The snake twists round a cactus,
As if he were tempting Eve to take an apple,
Eyes glow, watching every movement.

Listening to every sound
Until a desert mouse scampers to a
Different fort, running from the snake,
Tail vibrating, tongue flickering.

With a quick flash it's gone.

I checked my watch, it did not tick
The beat of my heart was the snake's tail rattle.

Alina Eisler (11)
Falkner House

Elephant

The forest opens
To my huge hoofing,
Ripe grass flattens
Under my lumbering stomp.

My trunk trumpets hoarsely,
Heaves logs,
Squirts water
At my dry skin's pleasure.

My tiny eyes, like marbles
Catch the darting lizard,
I long to be so small, so quick
So easily disguised to others.

Slung at my bulging back
Its flimsy ends frayed,
Made of metal string it hangs.
It is negligible.

Carefully flapping outwards,
Fanning my skin
My ears are gigantic
My personal air-conditioner.
As my tusks dig
The ivory is perfectly hooked,
Reflection has left them now,
The sky darkens.

Victoria Sassoon (10)
Falkner House

Squirrel

Squirrel is started . . .
She takes the orange of a pepper,
She takes the white of snow
To make her fur.

For her ears . . .
She takes the points of icicles,
She takes the pink of human skin,
She takes the flexibility of elastic.

From the strongest metal
She takes the power of an axe,
She takes the force of a twig
To make her feet.

For her eyes . . .
She takes the black of night,
She takes the shimmering of stars,
She takes the brightness of sun.

From the galaxy around us
She takes the engine of a rocket,
She takes the movement of a cheetah
For her motion.

For her actions . . .
She takes the stomp of a mouse,
She takes the energy of a leopard,
She takes the anger of the alligator.

For her tail . . .
She takes the fleece from a sheep,
She takes the length of half-grown corn,
She takes the velvet of moleskin.

Squirrel is started!

Farran Elvidge (9)
Falkner House

Panther

He creeps silently through long grasses, it rustles,
But not just by him, but by the wind too.
His eyes glow like two small moons,
Under the trees his eyes are green, and you can see
Them wide as slits in paper.
His claws make small dents in the earth,
But he hardly makes a sound.

He gives his black tail a flick as if he rules the world.
He finds a tall, sturdy Acacia tree.
He climbs up with care, and
Delicately leaps onto a branch that he knows well
For there are many scratches along the bark.
Leisurely he lies down and opens and closes his eyes.

His ears prick, his eyes open with a snap.
They are intense and focused this time.
He leaps from the bough and lands quietly.
On all four of his paws and he slinks away, near the stream
Which dribbles and it trickles and hits very slightly against a rock.
He takes a lap, from his whiskers, water drips off them.

He prowls away heading towards the long grasses,
Through the softer soil and creates,
A large paw print in his name.
As if he were wading into bulrushes, his
Body is half obscured but soon there is none of him to see
But the memory remains.

In the distance something flicks up out of the grasses
Like a big black cat's tail.

Marisia Nowak (11)
Falkner House

The Black Cat

Eyes like emeralds
Stare into space
Like rings of dangerous fire.

Whiskers black as coal
Twitch and quiver and shiver
Like a peacock's magnificent tail.

Tongue like a scouring pad
Rough and coarse
Like spears of silver.

Teeth like swords
Slice and tear
Through mouse flesh.

Tails whisk and whirl
And twirl and twirl
Like windmills spinning slowly.

Alexa Olsher (9)
Falkner House

My Cat Puddle

She stalks you with her green glass eyes
And you sleep well, knowing she's on patrol,
I gently rock her in my arms
Her purr is music to my ears.

She hides behind a tree to snare a blackbird,
Her whiskers twitch and quiver
Her teeth are razor-sharp,
You must feed her particular fish to make her feel happy.

Sometimes it seems like she dances
She will hiss like a snake when she's angry,
Her fur is soft as dandelion clocks
Tail like a skipping rope.

Ffion Dash (9)
Falkner House

India

Burning, hot country with temples and palaces,
Snakes slithering over the scorching hot sand,
People journeying towards the market,
Rivers fast flowing along the dry path.

Sweet smelling mangoes of orange and yellow,
Pineapples yellow and spiky and ripe,
Curries and spices, big wooden bowlfuls,
Fiery hot chillis and peppers bright red.

Stalls hung with saris silky and cool
Brilliant colours, turquoise and blue,
Rugs like mazes with amazing patterns
Rolled up and piled and tied tight with string.

Flowers lay in garlands in woven grass baskets,
Jasmine flowers smelling so fresh and so sweet,
Ivory elephants with carefully carved bodies,
Diamonds gleamed in the brilliant sun.

Charlotte Broadhurst (9)
Falkner House

Dancers By Degas

Silk bows dangle like apples from a tree,
Satin skirts glide through the air
A wreath of flowers falls from her hair;
Organdie ballet shoes point like thorns.

Her arms flutter like swans wings
She floats across the stage,
Her legs stretch like tree branches
She leaps as high as a dancing hare.

Flutes whistle like nightingales
As the violin swishes its bow across the strings.
Harps hum to the beat;
The cello howls like the wind.

Olivia Garner (9)
Falkner House

Sunflowers

Sunflowers glow
In the midday heat
Like sparks of fire in a marble hearth.

Amber, mustard, wax and bronze,
A palette of flowers
Bursting with colour in an August field.

Spiky petals wave in the wind
And turn to the sun
Like magnets to metal.

Their heads surprise me,
A present you thought you'd never receive.
They burn my soul into a maze of wonders.

Serena Joly (10)
Falkner House

Sunflowers

Sunflowers shine in a vase,
Colours rich and rare
Like golden jewels.

Yellow, orange, auburn, copper
Mixed on an artist's palette
To form a sunflower.

Petals flame in a jug
On a sunlit shelf
Like a fire-crackling plant.

When I see this flower
I think of a fiery furnace,
Burning metal melting into liquid.

Natasha Molson (10)
Falkner House

The Reef

Sun gleams on the sea's sapphire surface,
Splitting shadows into splinters.
The great sea breaks with the rhythm of music
Dipping, dashing, on the coral reef.

Shoals of shapes dart and twist
Turning, spirals of endless colour,
Shells, sponges and hoards of life.

Arrays of coral like a city,
Each a palace of natural beauty,
Slivers of light shine through sleeves of seaweed
Red and green, a forest of branches.

Sand, pure white, a carpet of silver
Where urchins rest on rocks.
Anemones wave their arms in peace
Where clownfish pass between.

Olivia Yallop (11)
Falkner House

Evening

Mum is in the kitchen, preparing dinner
For friends who are coming round.
It smells like steak.
Dad has just returned from work
I wish he would shut the door, it's freezing.
I forgot to feed the guinea pig.

As I walk out in my slippers
I catch the sudden chill,
I walk across the lawn, past the
Apple tree that looks like a giant Christmas spruce
Decorated with baubles,
Into the safe shelter of the barn.

Natasha Kelly (10)
Falkner House

Parrot

Parrot became,
She took shades of a rainbow
And shine of metal
To make her feathers.

For her voice . . .
She took the screech of a violin,
The squawk of a crow,
And the hoot of an owl.

For her talons . . .
She took the shape of a river's delta,
The round of a quarter planet,
The horn of a unicorn.

For her eyes . . .
She stole coal from the Earth's core,
A remnant of sky,
The glint of a star.

Parrot became.

Florence Rayner (10)
Falkner House

Spell From The Sea

A fleshy, poisonous jellyfish sting
Then a powerful seagull's wing,
Next a lock of mermaid's hair
Throw it in with extra care,
A cup of salty, thrashing sea
Long dried leaves from tall palm tree,
Catch a shiny oyster's pearl
A silver angelfish's tail;
Now a killer shark's sharp grin,
Put into a sailor's tin,
Drop them in and mix them well
To make a shining magic spell.

Isobel Cullinan (10)
Falkner House

In A Sailor's Pocket . . .

(Inspired by 'Magic Box' by Kit Wright)

A bright pearl sparkling in the sun
A photo of his little one,
A book to teach you about fish
A round gold coin to make a wish,
A cracked compass, broken down,
And fishing net he bought in town,
A white and sandy sailor's hat
A chocolate sponge cake squashed down flat!
A rusty key to fit a lock
A white line round a lucky rock,
Green seaweed that begins to smell
A ship in a bottle he's going to sell,
A picture in a very old locket
That's what I found in a sailor's pocket!

Rachel Branson   (9)
Falkner House

Granny's Pets

(Inspired by 'Magic Box' by Kit Wright)

In her cupboard Granny kept . . .

Ten Tamworth pigs snorting
Nine green lizards darting
Eight golden hamsters gnawing
Seven white mice scraping
Six dawn foxes prowling
Five black and orange tigers snarling
Four black gorillas scratching
Three pink flamingos standing on one leg
Two yellow snakes slithering
And . . .
One duck-billed platypus sulking.

Claudia Matthews   (9)
Falkner House

Mystery Cat

Eyes like gemstones
Green as emeralds
Piercing stare.

Teeth like needles
Catch and capture mice
Puncturing skin.

Tongue rough and gritty
Coarse and abrasive
Like sandpaper.

Whiskers like violin strings
Twitch and quiver
In small spaces.

Tail as tender as a swan's neck
Flows through your fingers
Like a river.

Georgia Jones (9)
Falkner House

The Wood

The wood is dark
So is the car park.

The wood has no light,
Which shines bright.

The wood is as creepy
As makes anyone freaky.

The wood is deep
And puts one to sleep.

This wood is deep
And spooky.

Tobi Jaiyeoba (9)
Leopold Primary School

In North London

I live in North London
Where nothing is common,
My brother's called Solomon
Thinks parks are foul.
You see he is a nutter
He values nothing,
And thinks ill of everything.
You would not like to meet him,
Maybe in a dream.

Riche Campbell (8)
Leopold Primary School

Dared! Scared!

If I am scared
It's because I dared
To do different things
From those all around you.
Should I dare?
Or should I care?

Neil Tucker (8)
Leopold Primary School

The Seaside

I like going to the seaside
When it is nice and sunny
And pretend I am a whale
With a very big tail
I make a sandcastle
With my friend called Listle
I really love the seaside.

Nia Deacon (6)
Leopold Primary School

Cinderella

Cinderella lost her slipper
When she went to the ball
The prince chased her,
Then he began to fall.

He looked around the city
He took the slipper with him.
Everyone thought what a pity,
He was so sad and grim.

The last house had the two ugly sisters,
Who tried on the slipper
Which didn't fit them.

A girl came up from the cellar,
Now the prince has found Cinderella.

Ismail Bashir (6)
Leopold Primary School

Opposites

Oh, my sister
She is a nightmare.
When I stand,
She sits.
I think when I cry,
She laughs.
When I am good,
She's bad.
Oh Mum,
She is a nightmare.
Stop her!
Teach her!

Ayan Nasir (8)
Leopold Primary School

Brothers

What happens
When I do something?
I get into trouble
When my brother does something,
No one cares.
My brother gets all the good stuff
When I am stuck with puff,
All because I seem to act
So! So! badly.

Simi Ogunsola (9)
Leopold Primary School

Face It

I'm writing in the classroom
It's nearly time to start
I wish there was a way to stop
The pounding in my heart.
The parents in the corridor
Are chatting cheerfully:
And now I've got to face them
And I'm nervous as can be.

Maleeha Sheikh (9)
Leopold Primary School

Games

I like football
My friend likes tennis
When I play I score a goal
When he bats the ball he misses
I think tennis is boring
He doesn't do much scoring.

Simeon Adesanya (6)
Leopold Primary School

Sibling

When I am scared, my sister is brave.
When I am up, my sister is down.
When I go left, my sister goes right.
When I am sad, my sister is glad.
When I am good, my sister is bad.
When I am crying, my sister is laughing.
When I am standing up, my sister is sitting down.
What a sister.
For such a brother.

Tolu Ogundana (8)
Leopold Primary School

My Baby Sister

My baby sister is nice
She has lovely blue eyes
I hug her and kiss her
And take care of her.
Some days she can be naughty
And hit me with her toys.
She puts my things in her potty
Then screams and makes a noise.

Kamiylah Fogah-Watkins (5)
Leopold Primary School

I'm Hungry

Mummy, Mummy, Mummy,
I am very hungry.
I have looked in the cupboard
But there is not any food.
I think I will go to Aunty
Where we can have a party.

Christian Hirani (5)
Leopold Primary School

The Bunny

A bunny took my purse
And ran away with the money
He gave it to the horse
The bunny said, 'He,he'
And laughed at me
But I didn't find it funny.

Kyra Foster-Bah (6)
Leopold Primary School

School

School is nice
School is fun
School is beautiful
School is wonderful
I like school
If there was no school
What could I do?
I really don't know.

Jordan Sen (5)
Leopold Primary School

Bunny Bunny

Bunny, bunny, where's my cat?
There he is under my hat.
Silently hiding away,
Keeping quiet with nothing to say.
But one, two, three, boo!
There you are, 'I see you.'

Edaina Felix (6)
Leopold Primary School

Lion

Lion, lion
King of the jungle.

Here is a poem
For you and me
Sleeping in the jungle
Eating in the jungle.

Playing in the jungle
Killing other animals in the jungle.
Lion, lion, king of the jungle.

Jayeola Ogiunsola (6)
Leopold Primary School

Little Bat

Little bat, little bat
Have you seen my cat?
'Your cat is in the kitchen
Teasing all the chickens.'

Little bat, little bat,
Have you seen my rat?
'The rat is on the rung
Playing with the mug.'

Kayne Sancho (6)
Leopold Primary School

My Friend

My best friend called Mark
Has a friend called Billy.
They go to the park
And play games that are silly.

Faith Agyemang-Lorainey (5)
Leopold Primary School

The Cat And The Rat

A cat just ate a rat
The cat saw a bat.

The bat was fat
And he sat on a mat.

The cat was as fat as the bat
The rat that the cat ate was fat
So that's what made the cat fat.

I saw the bat and the cat was fat.
They were as fat as a rat.

Charlotte Winkler (6)
Leopold Primary School

Enemy, Enemy

Enemy, enemy, can't we be friends?
Enemy, enemy, have seen enemies on the TV
Songs about enemies, raps about enemies and movies
Eight-legged freaks, seeing is believing.

White and black, they were enemies
Can't we be friends, can't we be friends?

Look at the world without our friends
Now that American Dream is not real to me.

Mansor Shillingford (8)
Leopold Primary School

Shopping

I went shopping with Mum
All she bought me was gum
I went shopping with Grandma
She bought me a car.

Ndea Lawrence (5)
Leopold Primary School

When I Was One

When I was one,
I ate a bun.

When I was two,
My face went blue.

When I was three,
I could not see.

When I was four,
I went to war.

When I was five,
I had a beehive.

When I was six,
I could mix,
But now I'm seven
I'm looking forward to being warm.

Fikayo Fagade (7)
Leopold Primary School

When I Was One

When I was one, I sucked my thumb
When I was two, I did a pee
When I was three, I was hardly me
When I was four, I was at the door
When I was five, I was alive
When I was six, I was able to fix
When I was seven, I was in Heaven
When I was eight, I was a gate
When I was nine, I went to dine
When I was ten, alive again
When I was eleven I went to Devon.

Canute Simpson (7)
Leopold Primary School

The Tsunami

I can see the fish in the air,
Screaming and shouting of the wave over here.
This is a nightmare but over the sea,
People are laughing, *hee, hee, hee.*
But I'm not laughing, this is not funny,
But I know, this is only a bad dream.

I can hear the tsunami strike,
People running left and right.
Children and adults dying,
Family and friends crying.
People getting washed away,
This was the most horrid day.

I feel sad that my friends have died,
People tell me bad things, but this one should be a lie.
This makes me feel like a girl going mad,
So I shout and shout and go mad.
I feel like I want to scream
And wish that this was a very bad dream.

Sedayah Jorja Simpson (8)
Leopold Primary School

What A Citizen

Once there was a little girl called Robben
She turned into a mug
Picking and steaming.
She turned into a rotten old slug
And has collected dirty rich stuff.
The law caught up with her
The police had cuffed her
What a life!
What a bad citizen!

Stefan Lindsay (8)
Leopold Primary School

I Won!

One morning I had a tennis match.
I was so excited I thought, *I'm going to hatch.*
Then I got dressed as fast as lightning
And my sister said, 'Frightening.'

When I got in the car
I thought the journey would be far
Mum got me ready
On that day she was walking, she wasn't steady.

When we got there
We got out of the car and Mum got a chair.
When I got on the court
I had a really bad thought.

'What if she beats me
Even seven-three'
When we started
I sprinted.

'Hey it's okay
I might not beat you anyway.'
When she hit the ball
I felt like I was going to fall.

When it came to six – two
I really needed to go to the loo
When I came back I was steady,
'Ready, ready, ready.'

When I took the winning shot
It went in, I got really hot.
'BJ you won! You won!
Now your match is done.'

When I went to get my medal
My dad phoned and said something's wrong with the kettle.
My mum was so happy
She went back to the car to change Nia's nappy.

When we got home everyone hugged me
I even got squashed by the key.
When I went outside to practice
I saw my friends and said, 'What is this total madness.'

I wish I could play all day
My coach said I could!
Hip, Hip, hooray!'

Brianna-Jade Lewis (9)
Leopold Primary School

Senses Family

Taste
My mother tastes as sweet as a sherbet.
My father tastes as sour as a lime.
My cousin tastes as nice as nuts.

Sight
I can see as good as a bat at night-time.
My grandmother can see as far as a telescope.
My auntie can see as acutely as an eagle.

Smell
My mother smells as sweet as the scent of a rose.
My father smells as rotten as the rubbish bin.
My cousin smells as sweet as a sunflower.

Feel
My grandmother feels as happy as a lark.
My auntie feels as lonely as a lion.
I feel as bright as a bird in the sky.

Hearing
My mother can hear as far as a rhino.
My father is as deaf as an elephant.
My cousin can hear as good as a musician.

Lumahl Okocha (10)
Leopold Primary School

What I Need

Cooking and working,
All day long,
I really need a dog.
When am I going to get one?
Now or then?
Will it be early? I need to know.

Running and jumping,
All day long,
I really need a toy.
When am I going to get one?
Now or then?
Will it be early? I need to know.

Looking and staring,
All day long,
I really need some glasses.
When am I going to get some?
Now or then?
Will it be early? I need to know.

Daniel Olugbola (8)
Leopold Primary School

Weather

The sun and the rain
Make the plants grow.
The wind blows,
And when it snows,
It blows harder.
The sun shines better
The rain falls more
The cycle continues.

Jauier McKetty (8)
Leopold Primary School

The Bully Awakes

The bully has awoken,
My mum bought me a token,
I walked down the road,
I selected another mode.

The bully awakes,
I heard an earthquake,
My mum said, 'Come back!'
But I refused that.

The bully awakes,
The bully acts like a fake,
When the teacher spoke,
The bully got poked.

The bully has awoken,
Jimmy McDonald he slept on,
Lips parted, eyes closed,
They're clearly gone.

Aaliyah White (9)
Leopold Primary School

Nonsense Rhyme

Sometimes,
Every kind of people,
Tease me
When I tell the teacher
They always please me.

When it's time for dinner,
There's always a killer,
When it's time for a food fight,
They can do it alright.

Malik Deacon (8)
Leopold Primary School

Bullying Me

Sometimes I am frightened,
Sometimes I am not,
People always bully me
And they say I have a beard.

I do not know what it is,
Maybe it's me,
Like Aunt Lee.

Some say I'm dumb,
Some say I'm not,
They always bully me,
But my friends,
Are more than the
            Bullies!

Jhané Imani Ormsby-Jackson (9)
Leopold Primary School

My Behaviour

School is fun
School is sometimes boring
Sometimes I am happy
Sometimes I am sad
I don't know,
If it's PE or the teachers
Giving me scares,
But I think
My behaviour is poor.
So teach me Mum,
To try to behave myself
Teach me,
Teach me.

Nazerine Graham (9)
Leopold Primary School

Disaster

Vibration causes giant waves
Flew far and fast as a flash
Running across the Pacific Ocean
Scaring people everywhere
Devouring and killing people.

Screaming children
Screaming, running everywhere!
Soaring higher and higher
Enveloping people
Seizing people, houses, everything.

Millions of people gone!
Families sad!
Mums and dads disappearing!
Orphans sad and distressed!

Courtnai Melville (10)
Leopold Primary School

When I Was One

When I was one, I had some fun.
When I was two, I used to be bald.
When I was three, I was still me.
When I was four, I went on the floor.
When I was five, I was still alive.
When I was six, I got fixed.
When I was seven, I went to Heaven.
When I was eight, I had one gate.
When I was nine, I was fine.
When I was ten, I had a hen.

Jade Williamson (6)
Leopold Primary School

Seasons

Water likes to tinkle, rivers are flowing,
Lots of flowers are growing and growing,
Silver bells like to ring,
Now it is spring!

The days are warm, even at night,
Flowers are pretty and bright,
The sun is burning hot,
I like summer a lot!

Autumn days are red and brown,
Leaves are steadily falling down,
The sun slowly turns from yellow to gold,
Before it's swallowed by cold.

The last leaves have floated off,
Poor, cold people have developed a cough,
As all the snow swirls through the air
And all the winter trees are bare.

Amy Winkler (8)
Leopold Primary School

When I Was One

When I was one, I could run.
When I was two, I was blue.
When I was three, I was me.
When I was four, I knocked on the door.
When I was five, I got stuck in a beehive.
When I was six, I picked up the sticks.
When I was seven, I almost went to Heaven.
When I was eight, I was late.
When I was nine, I was on a big line.
When I was ten, I was a big hen.

Rianna Hendricks (7)
Leopold Primary School

Tsunami Disaster

Big disaster, people dying
Houses are blown away.
Screaming children and families
Rushing everywhere, bodies still not found.

More to come, more to find
And more relatives to describe.
Cold, lovely families
Orphans still crying.

On the news
People take their last stare.
They have a few minutes to live.

Parents dead, Mum and Dad
Died from that disaster.
Tsunami has gone like a flash in a pan.
Leaving memories never to be forgotten.

Waneta Newell (10)
Leopold Primary School

My Butterfly

I once had a beautiful butterfly,
More beautiful than ever,
She flew round in the garden shining like silver.
One day she was sitting on a flower,
I found she was laying eggs,
I was so pleased with that,
I was smiling more than ever,
I rushed inside to see some more eggs,
And there they were hatching like a hen.
Some hatched quickly,
Some hatched slowly,
That was the best day of my life.

Iman Benazha (7)
Leopold Primary School

My Favourite Sports

I love playing my favourite sport.
I think it is the best,
But even though I like it, I need to have a rest.
My favourite sport is American football,
We all know it's the best
My favourite team is Dallas Cowboys
But they also need a rest.

I like just plain old football
It has never changed
I like it when players do a hat-trick
I think my dad is the best footballer
My favourite team is Arsenal
But they don't always win.

I also love basketball
The two points and slam dunks are great
Michael Jordan and myself are the best players
We're great
My favourite team is the Bulls.

I also like baseball
I like it when they swing and hit the ball
My favourite team is New York Yankees
And that's all.

Zion Chetram (9)
Leopold Primary School

When I Was One

When I was one, I had fun.
When I was two, I was blue.
When I was three, I was hardly me.
When I was four, I was much, more.
When I was five, I was hardly alive.

Siane Ashanti (7)
Leopold Primary School

The Island

I can see people riding on their surfboards
Which they can't afford.

Sunhats flying away in the Santana breeze
And the trees making me feel queasy.

Cold drinks running down people's legs
People saying this is like a peg.

I can hear palm trees falling on cafes
And people making lattes.

Boats going out to shore
But people rushing to get more.

Animals saying unusual things
For some onion rings.

I can feel being hot and sweaty
Because my name is Betty.

The sun is beating on me
And I feel so free.

Rochelle McLeod (8)
Leopold Primary School

My Tongue

I have a tongue as sharp as a razor.
It can cut through any nonsense.
People ask me how do I do it?

I have a tongue so slippery and fast.
It can lick a thousand stamps as quick as lightning.
People ask me how do I do it?

I have a tongue as dry as a desert.
It can break bricks as hard as iron.
They ask me how do I do it?
I say, I am . . .

Nathan Rhoden (10)
Leopold Primary School

Tsunami Disaster

Big wave slithering on land.
Killed millions of people.
Washing them all away.
Lots of people crying.
Through day and night.
Waiting for help.

Orphan in distress.
Looking for parents.
Waking up for help.
Waiting for help.
Night and day.

Need aid.
Need help to find their parents.
Pray for help.
All day long.
Waiting for help.

Mohamed Idris (10)
Leopold Primary School

A Good And Bad Day?

It was a good day in the park,
My friend and I were having a race.
It was not very dark
And I was leading, in first place.

I stopped and said, 'Time out.'
I wanted to do a bet.
Whoever will win when we're about
We will get soaking wet.

There had been a storm,
We were so frustrated.
We were not even warm,
But we were concentrated.

Paula Tudek (10)
Leopold Primary School

My Quiet Cat

Little cat, little cat, you are so sweet,
However you are, I keep you neat.
You go outside and play,
That's very fun, OK.

You feel happy,
I feel sad,
However we feel
We will always have a deal.

I hear you *miaow*
You hear me say, 'Ow!'
We hear everything together
We just say, 'Whatever!'

Annabelle Lognon (7)
Leopold Primary School

Tsunami

People masher,
Toy crasher,
People dying,
Orphans crying.

House smasher,
Quick dasher,
Everything gone,
There's no more sun.

Tsunami victims crying for help,
Donate some money to do so,
They're crying out
No doubt!

Yasmine Benazha (9)
Leopold Primary School

Pizza Boot

Pizza boot, pizza boot
Oh, I want a pizza boot,
Pizza boot, pizza boot,
I wish I had a pizza boot.

Cheese, ham, pepperoni or pineapple
I don't care even if it's apple,
It's of pizza boot, pizza boot
But I would really prefer beetroot.

Pizza boot, pizza boot
Oh, I want a pizza boot,
Pizza boot, pizza boot,
I wish I had a pizza boot.

I have to have it today
But I would prefer it yesterday,
I'm trying to look for it, up and down
I'm trying to look for it, all around.

Pizza boot, pizza boot
Oh, I want a pizza boot,
Pizza boot, pizza boot
I wish I had a pizza boot.

Now I've found my pizza boot
And they even had beetroot,
Thank you for finding my pizza boot
And now I'll give you some.

Akilah Barnabie (9)
Leopold Primary School

Holiday

Spain is my favourite holiday,
But Spain gives me pain
And in Spain it rains, all day.

Shana Chanel Osbourne (8)
Leopold Primary School

My Favourite Things

I like to play
I can play all day
When Mum says, 'Come inside!'
I go to hide
But then I say, 'It's not that fun, when I can't play!'

I ride my bike
That's what I like to do.
I ride in the park
And I always hear dogs bark.
It's not a nice thing to hear
But you should give them a scare.

I like to play with my toys
I sit with them all day.
My mum says, 'You should have a rest
You know before you like it so.'

I like playing on the swing
Everyone likes that thing.
I play on it twice a day
Then I say, 'Hooray!'
I go home and tell my dad,
That was very mad.

Jamell Christie (9)
Leopold Primary School

When I Was One

When I was one, I saw the sun.
When I was two, I nearly grew.
When I was three, I climbed up a tree.
When I was four, I opened the door.
When I was five, I knew how to drive.
When I was six, I knew how to mix.
When I was seven, I went to Heaven.

Dana Barnett (6)
Leopold Primary School

Holiday Dream

Having a good time
In a holiday dream
Swimming in the water
Exactly like I dreamed
Living in a wonderland.

Sometimes I think it is a scene
Living in a hotel with a big fat TV screen
When I go to dinner
They serve and clean and scrub
Every dish I may need.

But I wish it was real
But the only thing I do
Is sweep and clean
That's not a holiday dream.

Gianina Graham (9)
Leopold Primary School

Love

I love drawing, writing and colouring
I never hate anything
Not even my parents
Love is everything to me
Love is hard work
Love is appreciation
And I show it, I never hate anyone.

Sometimes I have tolerance and initiative
Sometimes, I don't
My love is everybody's love
So is theirs.

Tianna Charles (8)
Leopold Primary School

Making A Cake

Shaking and baking,
Making my cake,
My friend doesn't know what to make.
I asked her and helped her to bake with me,
But then she had to go home for tea.

When she got home,
She went to her secret dome
And played and played,
All alone.

So I was alone,
Playing on my own,
With no one beside me.

I wanted to go to Betty's house,
Because my house had a mouse,
I screamed and screamed off my head,
Until I went to my bed.

Nakira Phillips (9)
Leopold Primary School

I Wish . . . I Wish . . . I Wish . . .

I wish I was a princess,
I'd fill every finger with rings,
I'd have earrings, make-up and perfume
And lots of nice looking things.

I wish I was a pop star,
I'd dance and sing around,
I'd walk up every street
And pass everybody I meet.

I wish I was a celebrity,
I'd shake my bum like Beyonce,
I'd have a boyfriend
Then I'd have a fiancé.

Rianne Wright (8)
Leopold Primary School

I Wish . . .

I wish I was a singer,
I'd have all the expensive rings on my finger,
But all those autographs, they're not my type,
The people will want to climb up my drainpipe.

I wish I was a princess,
Rich and royal,
I don't want to drink tea,
So that's not the thing for me.

I wish I was a model,
A show-off, but no puddles,
All those camera flashes,
Will burn my lovely eyelashes.

I'm happy the way I am,
One day, I'll choose what's best for me,
So you wait, you'll see.

Rike Adeniran (9)
Leopold Primary School

Tsunami Kennings

Wave chaser,
People killer,
Life fighter,
Building destroyer.

Love hater,
Screaming children,
Orphans crying,
People dying.

Head smasher,
People drowning,
Home chaser,
Brick smasher.

Jadesayo Adelekan (9)
Leopold Primary School

If I Were A Duck

If I were a duck
I would *quack, quack, quack.*
I would swim all day across the lake and back.
I would waddle, I would prance,
If only I had the chance.
If I were a duck
I would *quack, quack, quack.*
Yes, if I were a duck
I would *quack, quack, quack.*
If I were a duck
I would love a rainy day,
I would skip through the puddles
If I had my way,
I would . . .

Anjelah Kugendra (7)
Leopold Primary School

Sally's Pets
(Based on 'Peter's Pets' by David Orme)

In her bedroom, Sally kept
Ten silly little cats, hiding
Nine spiders that scuttled and hid
Eight stupid dogs, shouting
Seven hamsters that snoozed in the cage
Six small, little pigs
Five tall Geraldine giraffes jumping up and down
Four monkeys jumping on the bed
Three pythons who lived in the outside part
Two donkeys who lived in the wardrobe
One, guess what? A big giraffe.

Oyinkansola Otukoya (9)
Leopold Primary School

Holidays

I love all my holidays,
They are very special to me,
I've been to loads of countries,
Mostly near the Caribbean sea.

Spain was one of my favourites,
I spent most of my time on the beach,
The ice cream in Spain was to die for,
My mum just put up her feet.

France was also good,
But it was also quite cold,
We stayed inside most of the time,
Thank you, Lord.

Jamaica was the best,
It was so cool,
I saw my family
And I swam in all the pools.

I would like to go to Cyprus,
I've heard it's very good,
I love my holidays,
I hope you do too.

Domonique Smith (11)
Leopold Primary School

Riding My Motorbike

Riding my motorbike,
Riding and grinding on my super motorbike.
I go so fast, all you will see,
Is my engine, going fast,
It beats a racing car
In a race.
It zooms to school
And everybody asks,
'Where did you get that kind of motorbike?'

Isaac Kizza (8)
Leopold Primary School

I Love

I love my family
Especially my mum
Because when we're together
We always have fun.

I love my friends
I have no best one
They make me feel better
Than a hot, sticky bun.

I love my school
I learn lots in class
To me, school is more interesting
Than how sand makes glass.

I love my house
My room is really nice
I try my hardest to keep it clean
Just so that I don't get mice.

I love my belongings
They give me something to do
My favourite toy is my cow book
When you press it, it says, *'Moo!'*

I love my baths
So bubbly and calming
Almost as good
As meeting Prince Charming.

Cassandra Parkes (11)
Leopold Primary School

Big Waves

Big waves are coming
Excited children shouting
Mums and dads crying.

Shamaree Wilson (9)
Leopold Primary School

Football

Football, football, is the best
It always, always beats the rest.
My favourite player is Ronaldinho,
He's as tough as bricks,
He flashes through the opposition like they're sticks!

I kick a football everyday,
It's one of those sports that you just have to play!
After my tea, I have a kick around,
I play with any football that can be found.

Why do you ask, is this my sport?
For saying that, I shall put you in court,
Because as far as I know,
Football, football, is the best,
It always, always beats the rest!
Yeah!

Haider Bashir (10)
Leopold Primary School

Playground, Playground

We have fun in the playground and more
Leopold is the playground that I totally adore
Humming or singing all the break long
It's not a racket when we join along.

We play on the monkey bar and hang, 'who is the longest'?
Some people say I am the strongest
We run up and down, tired we may be
But by next break time, we are full of energy.

In spring and in summer, the weather is hot
We play football, netball and basketball, the lot
In winter and in autumn, the weather has changed
The snow and the rain makes the place look deranged.

Venezia Justinne Pitter (10)
Leopold Primary School

The Playground

The playground is where I go to be free
I love it because it doesn't cost a penny or a P
I love swinging from frame to frame
It is so cool, it will never get lame.

I love playing with all my friends
It's much cooler than a Mercedes Benz
I love the breeze going through my hair
The lovely, cold, fresh, fresh air.

Imagine all the wonderful things you could play with
A playground is just something you have to live with
It's so much fun
And is for everyone.

So come to the playground
And jump up on the ground
Come and play
It's a lovely day.

Chika Njoku (10)
Leopold Primary School

A Winter Poem

As the rain falls down
I know it's winter
When the clocks go back
I know it's winter
When Christmas comes closer
I know it's winter
When snow comes down
I know it's winter
When I wear my hat and gloves
I know it's winter
When it's grey and dull
I know it's winter
When there's fog all around us
I know it's winter.

Bianca Courtney (11)
Leopold Primary School

All In Andy's House

A boy named Andy from Liverpool,
Got up to sit on a stool,
He sat on it all night, all day,
Eighty years passed away,
He is now an old man from Liverpool,
He now has a wife, named Kat,
Who went and sat on a mat,
When the time was two o'clock,
She got up to put on her socks
And stepped out to buy a cat.
One day the cat felt sick,
Got out of her basket to get a toothpick,
It poked her all day,
It frightened her away
And she went and scared a mouse named Dick.
One day, the mouse wanted to get out of bed,
Tried to get out, but bumped his head,
He caught amnesia
And ran to the freezer,
The cold freezer in Andy's house!

Zainab Jalloh (10)
Leopold Primary School

Cats

Small cats
Small and black
Fast and furry
Cuddly
Small and cute
Lovely and smart
He does not bark
He drinks water
But the only thing is
He lives in a cage.

Selina Dyer (9)
Leopold Primary School

Family

Our family comes
From many homes,
Our hair is straight,
Our hair is brown,
Our hair is curled,
Our eyes are blue,
Our skins are different
Colours too.
We're girls and boys,
We're big and small,
We're young and old,
We're short and tall.
We're everything
That we can be
And still we are
A family.
We laugh and cry,
We work and play,
We help each other
Every day.
The world's a lovely
Place to be,
Because we are
A family.

Ebyan Abdirahman (10)
Leopold Primary School

Laptop Computer

My laptop computer can download music, CDs and games.
Because it is nice and beautiful,
And it's good for children.
It's got English, maths and science to play on it.
I can play whatever activity I want.
And it is really nice.
It is really perfect.

Matthew Kayembe (6)
Leopold Primary School

My Family

Taste
My mother is sweet
My dad is bitter
My two sisters are sour
And I'm just butter.

Sight
My mum is hairy
My dad is just the same
My two sisters are
And I'm just normal.

Hear
My dad is a dragon
My mum is a rooster
My two sisters are tigers and dragons
And I'm a dog.

Smell
My mum smells like lemon
My dad smells like grapefruit
My two sisters smell like cabbage.

Touch
My mum's skin is silky
My dad's skin is rough
My two sisters' skin is like rock
And my skin is the same as my mum's.

Andrea Feyisayo-Odedina (10)
Leopold Primary School

The Skeleton

Our skeleton keeps us together.
Without it we'd be a bag of feathers.
It helps us move, it helps us to groove.
It's strong, it has joints.
It stays with us forever.

Oyabola Oyesoro (10)
Leopold Primary School

At School

When I run
And talk
My friend walks away.
When I want to eat
My friend
Pushes in front of me.

Even when I try
To look at him
He turns away
I try to play, he pushed
But he pushed me down.

He's bored
He smacks the bricks too
He had to leave the school
I found life much better.

Don Brown (9)
Leopold Primary School

My Sister

Dalia is sad
She is feeling bad
She's been left out
And I feel mad.

Giving Dalia this bad feeling
Makes me angry day and night.

Tell someone, Dalia
Someone you trust
Tell please, tell you must
Tell someone at last
Then you're sure to get help, fast.

Rania Saeed (7)
Leopold Primary School

Fun Poem

I hit my baby sister,
My dad said, 'Go to your bedroom and don't come out!'
So I got a sharp knife and slit the mattress open,
Monday, Tuesday, Wednesday, Thursday, Friday,
I didn't go to school,
It was quite a hard fit
With all those springs.

My dad saw me and said, 'Come downstairs for dinner.'
Then he said, 'Now you eat everything!'
So I did.
I ate the dinner and the plate.
I ate the knife and fork.
I ate the food tray
And I even ate the table.

And that's me having fun!

Tanya Sheree Stern (8)
Leopold Primary School

That Girl

I was that girl you always bullied,
The girl you used to say was silly.
I always came but you pushed me away,
So I constantly came back
And used to say, 'Don't let's fight, but be friends.'
And you guys laughed,
While the straight lines in my head turned to bends.
You always wanted to fight
And I hope you've learnt a lesson,
That now you shouldn't be aggressive.
Now you're at the bottom
And I'm at the top,
So the best thing I can offer you is my
Friendship.

Taiye Fashipe (10)
Leopold Primary School

Trees

Grey and bold
All alone
Cold and bold
Strong and sad
Haunched and bronzed
Branches all along
Bare with no hair
Green and brown
Leaves and bark
Buds and roots
It stands strong
By itself
Cold, with no friends
Flapping on windows
Cannot be trusted.

Miles Lindsay (10)
Leopold Primary School

Animals

Animals are different
I wonder why
Some are big
Some are small
Some exist
Some are extinct
Why are animals different?
Who knows? That's how they are
But some people care.
I do care about animals
Do you?

Brenda Mshiu (8)
Leopold Primary School

Flowers

There are many different types of flowers in the world.

Roses are red,
Violets are blue,
Some have beds,
Some have pots.

There are tall ones,
And there are small ones,
Scented and colourful,
Oh! here comes a bee,
Buzz!

Flowers for the bride,
Flowers for the dear ones who have died,
Flowers for all occasions.

Hanaa Bashir (7)
Leopold Primary School

Sammy Snake

Sammy Snake is so long,
Sammy Snake has a very long tongue.

Sammy Snake saw a rake,
Sammy Snake baked a cake.

Sammy Snake saw Tony Hawke,
Sammy Snake saw a hawk.

Sammy Snake saw a cheetah,
Sammy Snake made some Cheetos.

Sammy Snake saw a bike,
Sammy Snake saw a trike.

Sammy Snake went to bed,
Sammy Snake laid his head.

Joshua Parkes (8)
Leopold Primary School

Rose

Rose so sweet
Smell so deep
So beautiful and bright
To my delight
And my love is like
A red, red rose
That springs in June
I can made a candle
Out of it
It smells so sweet
And smells so lovely
And it's beautiful
Just like you!

Shemond Dale (9)
Leopold Primary School

Tsunami

Wave going up, up and up
To the sky
Oh my, it is coming down
Wet, wet, wet, sad
We don't want to run, run
Like the wind.

So many people dying
So many dads and mums
All the people are gone
Why can't it be good?
Make it a better world.

Benjamin Currie (9)
Leopold Primary School

Tsunami!

Tsunami! Tsunami!
The world is better without you
You took the children
Away from their parents
When you struck
You have been
Crushing people so badly
That children have been orphaned
I wish you would
Leave the world
In peace.
Tsunami!

Rowan Edwards (9)
Leopold Primary School

If I Was Something, What Would I be?

If I was something, what would I be?
I would be a bird and fly away,
Or maybe a horse and gallop someday,
Swing like a monkey, high in the trees,
Swinging as happy, as happy can be,
Maybe a snake or a lizard,
What's next?
Maybe a giraffe to see all around the world.
The one I choose as number one,
Is a horse galloping and having fun.

Cherelle Thompson (11)
Leopold Primary School

Fish

Running with no legs,
Oh, it's hard.
They say that's how I am,
Like a talking card.

Yes, they tease me,
Twenty-four-seven,
When they aren't around me,
I feel like I am in Heaven.

Why they tease me,
Nobody knows,
I bet you do,
It's right at the end of your nose.

The silliest thing,
They ever told,
Was that I,
Was a fish!

Reion Tibby (10)
Leopold Primary School

Write A Poem

Hey, everybody,
Let's write a poem,
First, there's a boy,
That looks like Owen,
He likes playing football,
But he always falls,
What's the point of playing,
If you have no training?
So train for everything,
Try writing a poem.

Aimen Idris (8)
Leopold Primary School

I Wonder

I wonder what will happen
If there was never any schools
Where would I learn to read
If there were no schools?

I wonder what would happen
If there were no shops
Where would I get a lollipop
If there were no shops.

Mathun Kuganesan (6)
Leopold Primary School

Tsunami

T is for tsunami
S is for Sunday, 26th December
U is for unhappy
N is for never coming back
A is for angel
M is for many people have died
 I is for in the sea.

Patrice King (10)
Leopold Primary School

The Man And The Rat

The man had a pet which was a rat.
But he sat on the rat
He bought a new rat which was a cat.
His name was mice
And he was nice.
His nice, new rat
Was like a cat.

Zahra Ahmedali (5)
Leopold Primary School

My Science Experiment

Sometimes, if you poke things in a socket,
The electricity might go into your body.

I know that batteries have chemicals,
That keep the power within bounds.

Get a bulb that is white
And plug it in at night,
It will set the place alight.

You can use electricity to play your Game Boy,
But it cannot bathe you.

Electricity is a source that flows in wires,
But be careful, because it can make fires,
Electricity is not bad, it can make our lives better.

Isobel Rose Adedeji (6)
Leopold Primary School

Chinese New Year

Rooster knows that it's his year to crow,
Coming tenth is his race, he is taking this place,
Representing this New Year 2005,
The dog comes next, yep, 11th is his place,
Even though he had come 11th in his race,
He has no loss of face.
Rat was very clever, he rode across that long river on ox's back,
When ox turned around, he made a sort of sound,
Cheering that he had won.
Rat then jumped off ox's back
And had taken the lead,
Then crossed the finish line.

Savannah-Rae Judith Wright (10)
Leopold Primary School

An Experiment

Last week I did an experiment with my class
And it was really good.

Now I think it is really useful,
Before, I used to think it was silly.

Now I know how electricity works
For cookers and computers.

I have learnt that batteries have chemicals
And electricity in them
And I learnt that we should not open batteries
Because of the chemicals.
When batteries do not work,
We should throw them away.

I have also experimented with circuits,
We did it for our assembly
And we showed the children how they worked
And they were amazed.

Now, I bet you want to know how the experiment worked.
Well, first we got a light bulb holder,
Then a battery and some crocodile clips.
Then you connect the crocodile clips to the light bulb holder
And the other end of the crocodile clips
To the positive and negative ends of the battery.
Then we got the bulb all aglow!

Layla Bradford (6)
Leopold Primary School

Somebody Loves You

Somebody loves you
       And wants you to know,
Longs to be with you
       Wherever you go.
Somebody loves you
       Right from the start,
Somebody wants to
       Come into your heart.

If you cannot
       Love somebody back,
You can have a
       Nice job and a flash car,
There is still something
       That you will lack.

If you can make room
       For someone in your heart,
You and
       Your loved ones,
Should never
       Part.

When you grow up
       You should always know,
If you
       Love someone,
You will arrive at the stop
       To which you want to go.

Jordan Raeburn (10)
Leopold Primary School

A Little Bit More

A little bit more of sunshine
A little bit more of rain
A little bit more of growth
A little bit more of wisdom
A little bit more of happiness
Flowers, blossoms, buttercups everywhere.

A little bit more
A little bit more.

A little bit more of praise
A little bit more of singing
A little bit more of dancing
A little bit more of worship
A little bit more of prayers
Flowers, blossoms, buttercups everywhere.

A little bit more
A little bit more.

A little bit more of love
A little bit more of care
A little bit more of kindness
A little bit more of peace
A little bit more of victory
Flowers, blossoms, buttercups everywhere.

A little bit more
A little bit more.

Abigail Abena Gyesi (10)
Leopold Primary School

Dangers Of Electricity

Electricity can be dangerous,
So don't be outrageous.

If you play with electricity
You will get electrocuted.

Do not play with wires,
Instead, play with tyres.

If you friends talk about wires,
Say, talk about tyres.

Electricity's very good
Because it's never in a mood.

Electricity can be good
Because you use it for laptops.

We use electricity every day
But don't put metal in a switch
Or you might end up like a witch.

Deborah Orukotan (7)
Leopold Primary School

Electricity

Electricity flows in a circuit
Electricity can be a danger
So never play with electricity.

If you put a plug in a socket
With wet hands, you can get electrocuted,
But electricity can be good.

Because we use it for the computers,
Torches and microwaves and other stuff.
If you put batteries the wrong way round,
There is a break in the circuit.
Never try to break a circuit.

Tyana Lynch (7)
Leopold Primary School

I See A Butterfly

I see a butterfly on a leaf,
Getting ready to get on her knees.

The butterfly laid some eggs, then she flew away
And I wonder if she would like to play.

Now, it's time to play,
But then it was time to fly away.

I was new and I flew and flew
And I heard the cows moo.

I went to fly
And I saw somebody wearing a comfortable tie.

I laid some eggs
And I hung them on my page.

My butterfly is called Layla
And her husband is called Mayla.

A butterfly is very nice
And she does not even like rice.

Louise Jesi (7)
Leopold Primary School

Don't Mess With Electricity

Electricity can be dangerous
So never play with electricity.

If you play with electricity
You might get electrocuted.

You can use it on TV
But you can't do PE.

Electricity can flow
But it cannot blow.

Siobhan Mitchell (7)
Leopold Primary School

The Butterfly

One day on a leaf, an egg was laid;
A caterpillar egg is in the shade,
Wait five days and in that same patch;
That little caterpillar egg will hatch.

Once the egg is broken,
The caterpillar eats it;
Then eats the leaf he's on.

Crunch, crunch, munch, munch,
As the caterpillar goes;
Increasing his weight as he grows.

Spin, spin, spin
For dinner he eats his skin;
From morning to late afternoon,
He wraps himself in a cocoon.

From winter through spring,
His metamorphosis will begin;
With the warmer season,
Completes his change.

It's spring and soon,
He will break out of his cocoon;
From a branch hanging high,
Drying his wing, for now he's
A butterfly.

Sassikia Jarrett (6)
Leopold Primary School

Electricity

Electricity can be dangerous, so do not play with it.
If you play with electricity, you might get electrocuted.
If you play with electricity, the wires will get loose.
Electricity is good for computers and televisions and lights.
Electricity is very, very good, but it can be bad as well.
So be careful what you do with it.

Daniel Otukoya (6)
Leopold Primary School

A Girl Called Rema

There was a girl named Rema
Thought she was the best,
Got into class
And hated spelling tests.

She wore glasses
Thought she was a geek,
Went home and found out
She was a Greek.

It was class assembly
Rema was too shy to talk,
It was her go
And did not know how to walk.

Her family thought she was very ugly,
Found out her name was Smugly.

Rema was dreaming going down a hole
Woke up, on her face was a mole,
She did not want to see
Only had a peek,
Found out it was bigger than her cheek.

Jamal Liam Brown (10)
Leopold Primary School

I Am A Butterfly

The butterfly lays some eggs
And then the eggs hatch
And it takes a long time to get out of its egg.
The caterpillar keeps eating and eating
And eating and keeps eating,
Until it goes into its cocoon
And when it gets out of this cocoon in spring
It becomes a butterfly and it flies away.

Dion Rene Upton (7)
Leopold Primary School

What Is My Favourite Thing?

My favourite thing is my PlayStation,
No wait, it's my football.
I have many football things.
My favourite thing is my basketball,
No, it's my football boots.

What is my favourite thing?
What is my favourite thing?

My favourite thing is my football kit,
No, it's my radio,
I have so many favourite things.
My favourite thing is my basketball shoes,
No, it's my Walkman.

What is my favourite thing?
What is my favourite thing?

I have so many favourite things.

Kanyin Fagade (11)
Leopold Primary School

Daydream

There was a girl called Jane
And she was on a Virgin plane.
I liked her style,
Cos it was worth the while.
I came to her house
To show her my shoes.
It was a good day
So I was in a good mood.
I just found out
When I knocked on the door
That this girl had a family of four.

Raphael Louis (11)
Leopold Primary School

My Pet Cat

I have a cat, her name is Lizzie,
She's active, but inside she is a nice kitty.

She is really fluffy,
Soft and cuddly.
She likes to climb trees,
She is always very clean and never has fleas.

She likes to sleep on mats
And chase lots of rats.
She likes to play in the sun
And when she's happy, I'm happy too which is fun.
She has emerald eyes
And you know when she's happy she smiles.

When she hears J-Lo she dances on her back legs,
Then she wakes me up when I'm sleeping in my bed.

And that's about my cat.

Nicole Charles (8)
Mitchell Brook Primary School

My Family And Friends

My family is cool, my family is fun,
We giggle all day and all night.
When I go to school I meet,
Nicole, Ricki, Irena, Talika and Shannon.
These are the people who I hang out with,
They are very careful about what they do.

My family is cool, my family is fun,
We giggle all day and argue all night.
My family likes sitting in the sun,
Whilst my dad and uncle drink some rum.
When we go on holiday, we laugh and giggle in the sun.

Zhane Finikin (8)
Mitchell Brook Primary School

Seasons

Autumn is when the leaves fall down
And nobody ever makes a sound.
It's quiet, it's sweet, just with silence,
But people come and spoil the silence.

Summer is when we go out to play,
We also have some lovely cake.
We eat ice cream to keep us cool
And it's fun when we don't go to school.

Spring is when the blossoms show,
The wind is careful when it blows.
The sheep have babies and people too,
They name their babies and who knows who.

Winter is when the sun is down,
But nobody is in the mood to frown.
Make snowmen and women too
And some people even put on shoes.

Autumn is autumn,
Summer is summer,
Spring is spring
And winter is winter and that is what it is to me.

Halima Akinyemi (8)
Mitchell Brook Primary School

Holidays

A holiday is a trip to the beach,
You need to bring a picnic with peach.
Everyone can pick seashells,
We can make a bell out of sand.

A holiday is a trip to the park,
My sister left a mark.
We can go on the swing,
The bag I forgot to bring.

A holiday is a trip to the fair,
I won a red tail.
We won a cat that miaowed,
I won a pretty crown.

A holiday is a trip to the seaside,
I went on a ride.
We bought some candyfloss,
My friends came across.

A holiday is a trip that's fun!

Ayodele Narh (8)
Mitchell Brook Primary School

Seasons

Summer is the time of year
When the sun shines warm and bright.
It is the most wonderful feeling.

Spring is when flowers bloom,
Throughout the year.
It is when the sun is bright
And when the world is a beautiful sight.

Autumn is when leaves turn brown,
It is when the trees begin to frown.
Autumn is when fall begins.

Winter is when the world
Is full of crystal-white snow.
It is when the sun feels ill.
Winter is when the cold wind blows.

Talika Pathiranage (9)
Mitchell Brook Primary School

He Who Owns The Whistle Rules The World

My intelligent big sister,
How annoying she is,
I can't stop kicking her,
She just teases me so much.
She sticks her tongue out
And I stick mine out back.
She does it again
And I punch her in the face,
But my mum, who has the whistle,
Can immediately stop the fight.

Katinka Achrafie (9)
Princess Frederica School

Moonlight

Moonlight shines on the world like a big torch
The moon slowly climbs over day
It shines over us like a gloomy face
Waiting for us to wake up
Then it moves on to the next country.

When the sun goes out
The moon takes over
The sea is scared of the moon's ray
Moonlight shines into your room
And into your eyes.

Moonlight shines over the world
And tells the sun to come out to play
The moon plays ping-pong with the stars
The moon is scared of the crowing cockerel.

The moon drops away like a drowsy man
The moon is like a vampire
It sucks away the day
And the moon dies when the sun rises.

The moon is king of the stars
It sits on its throne and looks over the night
The stars are its servants
And come out when it commands.

The moon is the king of the night
When he is out all is dark
The sun is scared of the moon
The moon takes away darkness and replaces it with light.

Tom Pomphrey (11)
Princess Frederica School

Night

She wore a gown of soft silk,
Her feet were clothed in gold,
Her eyes danced like sunny emeralds,
Glistening in the wind.

Her hands bore opals and diamonds white,
Her face was pure, but alone,
Her lips were red,
As red as fire,
Her hair dark brown and curled.

She wanders across the valley steep,
Dancing among the stars.
Riding on dragonflies,
Through the waters,
Her face drenched pale with sorrow.

She sets the dark
Aflame with fire,
A luminous light shines bright,
Her eyes resemble tigers',
Shining, oh shining
Like Hell's fire.

I met at ten,
The sorrowful thing,
We flew amongst the grass,
Her wings spread out,
She wore a smile
And out she flew,
Into the sky.

We said goodbye,
The night and I.

Ruth Bertulis-Fernandes (11)
Princess Frederica School

I Talked With The Troubled Night

I talked with the troubled night,
He responded like a little baby with a sweet, tired voice,
He said, 'Oh, please help me!
The stars are looking up to me for answers.'

I said to the night,
'The way you do it is to be the boss.'
The night responded by saying,
'But there are only little stars!'

Then I said, 'That's where you're wrong,
This is how you do it.
You've got to say, right listen to me,
If you have any questions
Come to me in a straight line.'

That night, when the stars were asleep,
The night came out to see me.
'How did it go?'
It was back to normal again.
'Thanks for your help, sir!'
'No problem! Just shout my name, night,
You know where I live.'

The night came to me and said,
'Why don't you come and visit us?'
And out I flew into the sky
And that's why, after dark,
The night comes out
And together we both dance among the stars.

Daniel Eugene (11)
Princess Frederica School

Tastes

Olives are salty and mousse is squelchy.
Crisps are bumpy and sweets are stretchy.
Chocolate's sweet, jelly is wobbly.
Marshmallows are squeegee, chips are treats.

Eya Taylor (6)
Princess Frederica School

Night

The night is wondrous
And wanders through the world,
With a whistle in the air,
Everyone knows its recursion.

With the moon in its hair,
Shining down on its face,
It looks like a twilight fairy princess,
With a smile as rosy as a happy girl.

It crawls through evening,
Until night,
Then morning comes and spoils its fun,
But tomorrow another night it will be!

The night gives a shine,
Like a man with well-brushed teeth,
It stands out,
From everything that ever existed.

The pool glows with brightness
And on the forehead
Of this wondrous thing,
A scary scare upon us falls.

The night is wondrous
And wanders through the world,
With a moan in the air,
Everyone knows it's gone.

Bruna Pereira (11)
Princess Frederica School

Tired

Tired is a brown mushroom and onion pizza.
It tastes like cheese.
It would smell of spicy herbs.
It looks like a round wheel.
It feels like a radiator cooling down.

Fergus Leahy (7)
Princess Frederica School

When It's Dark

When it's dark, I hear gentle tapping on the windows,
You can hear gunshots,
You can see the sky's blackness, darker than my hair,
You see the bright moon.

When it's dark, I hear people walking on the street,
You can hear drunken people,
You see the shadows moving,
You can see people running, like they've done something.

When it's dark, you see drunk drivers,
You can hear them rev the engine,
The engine is rumbling
And it's loud.

When it's dark, I hear people screaming,
My legs are wobbling
And sweaty,
I get frightened.

When it's dark, I see fireworks going up
And I hear the fireworks taking off.
They are very bright and beautiful,
I feel like they are going to hit me.

When it's dark, I can't sleep!

Sashi Halai (11)
Princess Frederica School

Mad

Mad is red.
Mad tastes like rotten cabbage.
Mad looks like you are pulling someone's hair.
Mad sounds like a boy screaming.
It smells like a dustbin.
Mad feels like my mum telling me off.

Tyan Thompson (8)
Princess Frederica School

Taste

Olives are smooth.
Bread is full of wheat.
Chips are made of potatoes
And chicken is delicious to eat.

Toast is crunchy.
Bacon is a type of meat.
Apples are sweet
And oranges are good to eat.

Mackenzie Madley & Simhika Pindoria (6)
Princess Frederica School

Anger

Anger is dark purple.
It tastes like slime and smells like honey and apple.
Anger looks like green mushy peas.
Anger sounds like *you!*
And it feels like you are done for.

Rebecca Thomsen (8)
Princess Frederica School

Tastes

Apples are juicy.
Broccoli's fluffy.
Meat is nice
And chicken's stuffy.

Spaghetti is curly.
Ice is cold.
Grapes are small
And ice lollies are cold to hold.

Jessica Pallone & Esme O'Dowd (6)
Princess Frederica School

Tastes

Olives are smooth.
Bread is full of wheat.
Chips are made from potatoes
And they are nice to eat.

Bananas are squishy.
Apples are juicy.
Ice cream is cold
For a girl called Lucy.

Tye'ronn Thomas & Ethan Tyrer (7)
Princess Frederica School

Love

Love is red,
Love tastes like red strawberries,
Love smells like flowers,
Love looks like roses,
Love sounds like rain,
Love feels like your mum and dad kissing you.

Rose Conroy (7)
Princess Frederica School

Tastes

Crisps are crunchy
And nice to eat,
Chicken is tasty
And it's meat.

Sweets are sugar,
Potato is nice,
Noodles taste yummy
And it's rice.

Tamara Gordon (7) & Omari Maxwell (6)
Princess Frederica School

What Is Green?

Green is a wet, shiny frog.
Green is the crunchy apples.
Green is a very hungry crocodile.
Green is the long grass.
Green is the beautiful trees.
Green is the wavy leaves.
Green is the little plants.
Green is the murky waters.
Green is a pretty colour.
Green is the juicy apples on the tree.

Jessica Ladhani (6)
Princess Frederica School

What Is Green?

Green is the leaves swishing in the wind
Green is the apples in the trees
Green is the grass swishing
Green is the slimy frogs in the pond
I like green
Green, green
Green, green, green.

Matthew Lyons (6)
Princess Frederica School

Mad

Mad is *red.*
It tastes like cold mushy peas
And smells like oily fire.
Mad looks like a big, dark factory.
The sound of echoing noise,
Mad makes *me angry!*

Jordan Grant (7)
Princess Frederica School

Tastes

Broccoli is furry.
Meat is sweet.
Chips are potatoes.
Fish is nice to eat.

Lollipops are very icy.
Ice cream is cold.
Meat is wicked.
Nuts have mould.

Solo Shariff-Hickey (7) & Kieran Kerr (6)
Princess Frederica School

Alone

Alone is red.
It tastes like cabbage
And smells like a horrible death.
Alone looks like a graveyard of people staring into the night.
Alone sounds like a burglar coming towards me.
Alone makes me feel scared.
I hear footsteps. Beware!

Celia Stolper (7)
Princess Frederica School

Tastes

Pizza is cheesy.
Peas are sweet.
Chicken's nutritious.
Peanut butter is tasty to eat.

Olives are sweet.
Bananas are squashy.
Rice is hot
And mousse is messy.

Naomi Hephzibah (6) & Caelum Allett (7)
Princess Frederica School

Tastes

Jelly is sticky,
Sweets are tasty,
Crisps are crunchy,
Chocolate is chewy.

Olives are strong,
Mousse is sticky,
Curry is hot,
Chips are crunchy.

Yanik da Costa (6)
Princess Frederica School

Furious

Furious is red.
It tastes like a bullet going through my mouth.
It smells like a rocket launching.
It looks like people fighting in World War II.
It sounds like a baby screaming to be fed.
Furious makes me think of fire.

Giacomo Luke (8)
Princess Frederica School

Madness

Madness is red and black
And tastes like black, burnt pies.
Madness is the smell of cold sheep's blood
And sounds like huge screams.
Madness looks like a huge bonfire with red streaks.
Madness is pure anger.

Peter Batchelor (8)
Princess Frederica School

Tastes

Olives are salty
Chocolate is hard
Crisps are to eat
Sweets are sweet.

Mousse is creamy
Mousse is squishy
Crisps are crunchy
Crisps are bumpy.

Carl Sakyi (7)
Princess Frederica School

I Am A Book

I am a book,
People like to read me.
Sometimes I am funny,
Sometimes I am not.
I have a lot of pictures.
Sometimes I have colour,
Sometimes I don't.

Honey Hodgson (7)
Princess Frederica School

Sad

Sad is red,
It tastes like burnt fox legs.
It smells like a stick burning.
It looks like a ghost coming to scare me.
It sounds like a giant coming to eat me.
It feels like red liver.

Almarn James-Downes (7)
Princess Frederica School

He Who Owns The Whistle Rules The World

My annoying older sister,
She bosses me around,
Her hair's like a bush
And she looks like a hound.
She snores like my dad
And I slave her like a queen,
She's an angel at school
And even a darling at home.
My mum never notices,
She says she's an angel,
But when she blows the whistle,
I have to come to her quick
And lie about what she said.
So I think it is just
She who owns the whistle rules the *world*.
Just *jokes!*

Isabella Adams (9)
Princess Frederica School

Bees

Bees, bees, buzzing bees flying through the air,
Bees, bees, buzzing bees flying here and there.
Bees, bees, buzzing bees make honey to fill my tummy,
Bees, bees, buzzing bees make honey that is yummy.
Bees, bees, buzzing bees flying up, up in the air,
Then down, down, zooming through the air.
Bees, bees, buzzing bees coloured yellow and black,
Bees, bees, buzzing bees are now on the attack!

Zachary Dagnino (9)
Princess Frederica School

The Black Night

It's got hair as black as paint,
It makes you feel so scared,
There is no hope to save you,
Run back home, run back home.

It's got a twilight, bright face,
Like a fairy princess,
You could watch it all night long,
It lures you out into the street.

The night runs over the day,
Like a giant tractor,
You don't want night,
Go away, go away.

The moon glows white as a sheet,
But still it won't go back to day,
Hours pass by, you can't sleep,
The shadowy night won't change.

The windy, wet night is coming again,
It's becoming very dark,
The misty night whistled a muffled tune,
Stay home, stay home.

It's got hair as black as paint,
It makes you feel so scared,
There is no hope to save you,
Run back home, run back home.

Sarah Mahfouz (11)
Princess Frederica School

Tastes

Chocolates can be crunchy.
Ice cream's cold and hot dogs are not.
Pizza is cheesy.
Bananas can be cooked in a pot.

Kori Morrison & Jenna Ladhani (6)
Princess Frederica School

Night

Night is cold and lonely
It departs when daylight appears
The air was sour for its breath.

Night is frightening and scary
A mystical, glittering figure
It always gives you goosebumps.

As I stare into the dark sky
I feel a certain touch
The night breeze is lovely and calm.

Her eyes were pale, a luminous light
Like sparkling opal diamonds.

Her feet were bare, but shone with gold
Her hair fluttered in the cool breeze
She smiled at me
And waved her soft, delicate fingers.

I followed on
But every time I look into the skies she's there
But now she has disappeared
Into the cold, dark and lonely night.

Hannah Eugene (11)
Princess Frederica School

Cheetahs

Some are slow, but most are fast,
They sneak up slowly in the grass.
Their pretty fur shines in the sun,
They look so swift as they run,
But the sun doesn't burn their lungs.
Sometimes they go ballistic,
But it's always realistic.
Sometimes they burst,
But you wouldn't like to see them at their worst.

Nico Nurse (9)
Princess Frederica School

Tastes

Olives are salty
Chocolate is yummy
Crisps are crunchy
Fill my tummy.

Mousse is creamy
Ice cream is cold
I will eat chocolates
When I get old.

Neah Shim-Hue (6)
Princess Frederica School

Tastes

Crisps are crunchy,
Jelly is slippery,
Sweets are chewy,
Chocolate is nice.

Mousse is creamy,
Olives are salty,
Noodles are tasty,
Ice cream is cold.

Ethan Wallace-Bowling (6)
Princess Frederica School

Happiness

Happy is light,
Happy tastes like fish and chips,
Happy smells like flowers
Happy looks like a park
Happy sounds like birds singing
Happy feels like everyone is together.

Esme Stanford-Durkin (7)
Princess Frederica School

A Mystical, Glittering Figure

I met a mystical, glittering figure,
Whose hair was as soft as silk,
As her warm eyes smiled at me,
She greeted me with a curtsey.

Her feet were bare, but shone like gold,
The air sour for her breath,
Her eyes were pearl, but lit the way
And her embroidered dress fluttered in the wind.

Her house in the valley steep,
With glittering, misty walls,
Her cheeks red and rosy
And her skin covered with diamonds.

Her voice was soft and sweet,
Her necklace made of daisies,
She danced through the waters
And sang among the stars.

I met a mystical, glittering figure,
Whose hair was as soft as silk,
As her warm eyes smiled at me,
She waved at me goodbye.

Laura Achrafie (11)
Princess Frederica School

Tastes

Sweets are sticky,
Chocolate is smooth,
Crisps are crunchy,
Olives are strong.

Sweets are crunchy,
Chocolate is sticky,
Ice cream is creamy,
Noodles are creamy.

Jovarn Blair (7)
Princess Frederica School

What Is Green?

Green is a crocodile that is angry,
Green is the leaves swishing in the wind,
Green is the colour of apples,
The green leaves are rustling in the tree,
A green caterpillar that wriggles around the tree,
A green fish wiggling around,
A dragon that is green,
A slimy frog is green.

Nico Toumazou (6)
Princess Frederica School

Dolphin

The swirly dolphin lightly moves on top of the glistening water,
Swirls until it is dizzy.
Into the blue water the lovely dolphin goes,
Speaks its special dolphin language.
I wake up in my small bed,
Wondering if it was a magical dream.

I realised it was not a dream,
I looked down at the sea
And there was the bright dolphin
Waving with one of its fins.
I felt so happy, I opened my window and said,
'Will you come again?'
The dolphin said, 'Yes, I'll come again.'
As soon as the dolphin went,
I settled into my small bed,
Still thinking about the great ride I had.

Miah-Rose Banfield-Cooke (8)
St Leonard's CE Primary School, Streatham

My Games Table

I got my games table for Christmas
I like it very much
When my cousin Jayden comes over
He says, 'Ah, Rhys, what a touch!'

My games table is quite big
It sits in the middle of my room
It can change to pool, football, air hockey
And to basketball.

Pool is the best, football is the second,
Basketball the third and air hockey fourth,
But I like them all, they are all very cool
You need to learn how to aim the ball.

Rhys Warner (8)
St Leonard's CE Primary School, Streatham

Lost In Space

Lost in space
I can't find my way out
I saw some aliens
It really freaked me out.

The aliens were scary
It was frightening
I went *aahhh*
And they went *roar.*

When I returned to Earth
I felt safe and warm
My friends asked me
'Have you been up to space again?'

Dayleth McKenzie-Manning (8)
St Leonard's CE Primary School, Streatham

There's Monsters In My House

There's monsters in my house,
They're growling all about,
They're chewing on my toys
And making a weird noise.

I'm getting very scared,
I'm hiding under the stairs,
I think I know what to do,
I'll hit them with bamboo.

Then they will be dead
And I can go to bed!

Laura Nasrin (8)
St Leonard's CE Primary School, Streatham

Colours

Blue is for the sky that is way up high,
Gold is for the glistening sun,
Purple is for the plums that are ripe,
Silver is for the moon,
Orange is for the exciting days,
White is for the snow,
Green is for the grass that grows
And pink is for the sunset at the end of a day.

Eloise Scoley (8)
St Leonard's CE Primary School, Streatham

Mad About Fat Joe

There was an old lady called Moe,
Who loved singer Fat Joe.
She said, 'Kiss me you fool.'
'Are you mad? I am cool.'
Then he went where she would not know.

Shahid Miah (11)
St Leonard's CE Primary School, Streatham

Oh, I Wish . . .

Dragons are scaly,
Dragons are bumpy,
Dragons are slimy,
Dragons are grumpy.

Dragons are fierce,
Dragons are mystical,
Dragons are enchanting,
Dragons are fascinating.

Dragons blow fire,
Dragons screech,
Dragons can be wild,
Dragons might have wings.

Dragons are tall,
Dragons are small,
Oh, I wish, oh, I wish . . .
I could take one to school.

Jahid Miah (7)
St Leonard's CE Primary School, Streatham

Summertime

Summertime has just begun,
The clouds have gone, it's time for fun.
The sun has come to say hello,
I know where I want to go.
Maybe the park, maybe the fair,
As long as it's fun, anywhere.
Hear the birds singing loud,
See the ants looking proud.
It's dinner time, time for food
And everyone is in a good mood.
The moon has come to say hello,
I've been where I wanted to go.

Nieka Payne (8)
St Leonard's CE Primary School, Streatham

Fairy Poem

Fairies like to dance and sway,
Fairies like to flutter away.
Fairies are very nice,
They like to eat star special rice.
Fairies like to sprinkle dust,
Fairies like toasted crust.
On the fairies' special day,
They all like to swing and play.
So now you know what fairies are like,
If you look up, you'll know you're right.

Ruby Arscott (8)
St Leonard's CE Primary School, Streatham

The Man Of Peru

There was an old man of Peru,
Who dreamt he was eating his shoe.
He woke up in the night,
With a terrible fright
And found it was perfectly true!

Lucy Allen (10)
St Leonard's CE Primary School, Streatham

Swimming In The Sea

A shark is what you don't want to see,
When you are swimming in the sea.
They swim around just looking for prey,
If you saw one, you would quickly swim away.
Their fin is big and their teeth are sharp,
You must never go swimming in the dark.
So please be careful when you are in the sea,
Because a shark is what you don't want to see.

Jéan-Paul Rama (8)
St Leonard's CE Primary School, Streatham

Rainbow, Rainbow

Rainbow, rainbow
Colourful rainbow
You brighten the skyline
With your wonderful colours
Bringing joy and peace
And the promise of a pot of gold
Rainbow, rainbow
Colourful rainbow
Never stray too far from me.

Zainab Olaoye (7)
St Leonard's CE Primary School, Streatham

At The Park

On Saturdays, me and my family go to the park
Baby Sasha plays in the sandpit
Thomas plays with the dog
Mum and Dad are talking
And me . . .
My bike is stuck in a bog!

Luka Kenyon (8)
St Leonard's CE Primary School, Streatham

At The Beach

I love it at the beach
The wind whistles through the air
The gentle breeze blows through my hair
Yes, I love it at the beach
Playing in the sand, what a lovely thing to do
Now all I need to have some fun
Yes, all I need is you.

Clemmie Kenyon (8)
St Leonard's CE Primary School, Streatham

The School Poem

Jazz and I are cool,
But what are you?
Are you a smart kid wearing jewels,
Who goes to school, which is cool?
Because Jazz and I would like to be your friends in school,
We are students in the class.
Today we are learning about instruments made from brass.
Our teachers are weird, but are clever,
Every time our teachers talk on forever.
But when you enter the class,
Our teacher thinks she can test us,
Because she says we are her tasks.

Krishen Patten (10)
St Leonard's CE Primary School, Streatham

Spring Is Coming

Oh, spring it is coming,
Oh, spring it is near,
Oh, I just can't wait until flowers appear.
Oh, spring it is near,
Oh, spring is just coming right here.
Sunflowers are bright as bright as a light,
They make me come right near.
Oh, spring it is coming,
Oh, spring it is near,
This poem is finished,
So bye bye, my dear.

David Gyamfi (8)
St Leonard's CE Primary School, Streatham

My Fat Cats

Scratching on our sofa,
Scratching on our chairs,
My fat cats,
Charge up and down the stairs.

Muddy paws on all the duvets,
Drive my mummy mad,
Muddy paws on all the pillows,
Make the children glad.

'Hooray, hooray, hooray,' they cry,
'No bed for us tonight.'
But Mummy cleans the sheets and pillows,
'Time for bed, sleep tight!'

Olivia Santoro (7)
St Leonard's CE Primary School, Streatham

Baby's Coming!

'Baby's coming,' Mummy shrieks,
It sounds like it will last for weeks.
Baby's making such a noise,
I think I'll go and hide my toys.

'Baby's coming,' Mummy shrieks,
Tears running down her cheeks.
Doctor's rushing all around,
I'll sell Mum's baby for a pound.

'Baby's coming,' Mummy shrieks,
It sounds like she is eating leeks.
Pins and needles in my feet,
Baby's sleeping on the sheet.

Bethan Powell (8)
St Leonard's CE Primary School, Streatham

Painting

Painting can be fun
My favourites are blue and red
The baby crawled right up the stairs
Tipped the bucket over and it hit Dad on the head.

'I've finished painting now.'
Dad shouted at me and said,
'No, no, you've done it all wrong!'
And hit me round the head.

Joel Bennett (10)
St Leonard's CE Primary School, Streatham

Six Little Bears

One little bear jumping in the hall,
Two little bears bumping their basketballs.
Three little bears playing in their school,
Four little bears having a call.
Five little bears eating their honey,
Six little bears cuddling their bunnies.

Samira Haque (7)
St Leonard's CE Primary School, Streatham

WWII

There are guns firing,
People dying
And big explosions destroying tanks.
Injured soldiers
And terrible sights,
I wish I'd stayed at home.

Laurence Balfour (7)
St Leonard's CE Primary School, Streatham

The Lean, Mean, Killing Machine

Twitchy nose
Long, thin tail
White-tipped.
Three kinds of ears
The bat, the cross, the flip.
Long, thin nose
Long, thin legs
Long, thin body come to that.

Like a bullet
Like a rocket to the sun
Or a man on the run.
A ball from a bat.
She crouches
She bounces
She jumps and turns
She's just as fast as a jungle cat come to that.

Razor-sharp teeth
Huge, gaping jaws
Seem to resist the claws
Of a squirrel or a cat.
Bite down on their necks
Foxes and rabbits
Shake them to death
With blood dripping from long tongue.
She's off again on the run.

Aeron Holland-Lewis (8)
St Leonard's CE Primary School, Streatham

The Young Lady From France

There was a young lady from France,
Who was given a chance to prance.
She now gave it all up,
That was some great bad luck
And now she can only just dance.

Portia Baker (11)
St Leonard's CE Primary School, Streatham

World War Two

Many soldiers went to war, fighting for their lives,
Trying to save their children's homes and their wives.
Germany lost and England won,
Germany surrenders, it has just begun.
Who got medals, who did not?
What sort of weapons have they got?
Deep underground the soldiers hide,
As their enemies come approaching from each side.
Arrows fly in the sky,
Children die from poisoned sweets,
Terrified birds start to tweet.
The war has ended, something was defended
And once again there are peaceful, loving people.

Roisin Ellis (7)
St Leonard's CE Primary School, Streatham

The Golden Sun

The sun is like a golden pot,
The sun is very, very hot.
The sun is very bright,
The sun is just right.
The sun is very fun,
The sun can't run.
The sun has far to go,
The sun is very slow.
The sun hurts your eyes,
The sun melts pies.
The sun likes to play,
The sun ripens the hay.

Rose Leach (7)
St Leonard's CE Primary School, Streatham

Ten Little Monkeys

One little monkey biting a tree,
Two little monkeys splashing with me.
Three little monkeys scared of the dark,
Four little monkeys playing in the park.
Five little monkeys in a beehive,
Six little monkeys about to arrive.
Seven little monkeys going for a swim,
Eight little monkeys training in the gym.
Nine little monkeys standing in a line,
Ten little monkeys feeling just fine!

Benjamin Allen (7)
St Leonard's CE Primary School, Streatham

Wrestler Limerick

There was a wrestler called Kurt
Who always in the ring got hurt
Acted like a baby
He would drink some gravy
He would then smash his face in dirt.

Keenan Trotman Guy (10)
St Leonard's CE Primary School, Streatham

Footballer

There was a footballer, Rooney,
He had a grandson called Mooney.
He looked a lot like Shrek,
But had no neck,
He had a wife called Looney.

Elliot Whitely (10)
St Leonard's CE Primary School, Streatham

Untitled

Icing cakes!
Mum, I will surely make a mess.
There's icing on the window
And icing on the floor,
There's icing in the front room
And icing on the door.
There's icing on the sideboard,
Whenever I put icing on the cakes,
There would have been icing on the plate.
I always make a mistake.
Sorry Mum.

Renece Harrison (11)
St Leonard's CE Primary School, Streatham

Beach Off

There was a young lady called Jade,
Who hit a boy with a spade.
When he had got told off,
She ran to the loft,
Then did the same thing to the maid.

Jade Licorish (10)
St Leonard's CE Primary School, Streatham

Cats

There was an old man from Delhi,
Who married a woman smelly.
They had a dozen cats,
That sat on purple mats
And all their names began with Telly.

Rhiannon Whitely (10)
St Leonard's CE Primary School, Streatham

The Rider

Hippity hoppity gibbery gee
Jumping on with lots of glee
Legs astride, knees kept tight
Reigns in hand, holding tight.

On my command, walking on,
Down the lane we ride
Squidgy, squelchy, through the mud,
Birds flying off to hide.

In a field off we go,
Rising up and down we trot,
Gently pulling back my reigns
I'm coming to a stop.

Through the bushes and the brambles,
Leaning down on the pony's neck,
Guarding my face while I smile,
The ponies follow in a single file.

Off we go, we start to trot,
Bobbing up and down,
As we canter, wind in hair,
Feels like we're flying through the air.

Annie Clarke (9)
St Mary's RC Primary School, Kilburn

The Human Body

A body, what an incredible machine.
It has a heart for pumping blood,
So that it will not flood.
It has lungs that are longer than tongues.
It has muscles which are for movement,
So that you can walk and run
And a liver is like a river,
That produces bile.

David Twumasi (10)
St Mary's RC Primary School, Kilburn

I Dare You

What would you do if your sister pulled out her hair?

Would you just sit and watch her doing the dare?

Or would you tell her to stop being a fool
And to go outside and swim in the swimming pool?

I would just sit and watch her doing the dare
And say to myself, *if she tells me off, I don't care.*
The sun is shining outside and I wish I could go out,
My parents have grounded me now you know what this is all about.

So here I am sitting and watching her
Wishing I could go outside and play with Max
I asked him to send me a fax but he said, 'No.'
My mum is a journalist and my dad is a scientist
That's why we all live on Mars!

Jessica Assaad (11)
St Mary's RC Primary School, Kilburn

Alarm

There was a young man called Peter McMarth,
He woke up one morning and went in the bath,
He phoned into work and said he'd be late,
As he forgot to turn the alarm to eight.

When he got into work,
He got a good old bellow,
Everyone felt sorry for the little fellow,
But he only wanted to see his best friend Kirk.

As soon as work finished, he went straight home
And had a long chat on his mobile phone.
He talked for a while and that made him calm,
But then he went to change his alarm.

Grace Horan (11)
St Mary's RC Primary School, Kilburn

Tiger

Tiger was our kitten a long time ago
Now I am lonely with no one to play.
You were so cute and cuddly
Always wanting to climb up high
You made us all laugh and cry.

But sadly one day you were taken away
We called out your name on that summer's day.
We searched and searched around the square
We asked all the neighbours and people there
But Tiger, oh Tiger, where did you go?

I hope you are somewhere safe and sound
With lots of friends to play around.
Tiger I will always remember you
As a happy and mischievous little kitten
Remember that time you got stuck in a mitten.

Nicole Mendes (10)
St Mary's RC Primary School, Kilburn

Iguana Rap

Beside the sofa sits So-Sophia,
My iguana loves ripe bananas,
She'll rap, rap, rap on my school skirt lap,
Flick out her tongue and when she's done,
She'll cruise to sleep in the deep, deep heat,
From the lamp inside her tank.

Under the sofa sits So-Sophia,
My iguana hates pet dogs.
She'll nap, nap, nap in a tiny gap,
Crawls out with ease with a bit of cheese,
Then cruise to sleep in a deep, deep heat,
From the lamp inside her tank.

Chloe Wilkins (10)
St Mary's RC Primary School, Kilburn

Dog

A dog, what a fantastic creature,
Looking for food and new tricks from a teacher,
'Cause if he didn't have you,
He would have nothing to do.

Look at him as he fetches his ball,
Sniffing a dog's butt,
Or catching something tall.
Even though he acts like a nut,
I think he's cute when he sleeps in his little doggy hut.

And when you get in that door,
He's there waiting for you,
And he jumps for joy and on you too,
Even if it makes you sore.

Connor Spaans (10)
St Mary's RC Primary School, Kilburn

Keen Nadine

There once was a girl called Nadine
Who was always so very keen.

Keen to be mean
Keen to be seen
Keen to be almost everything.

She was keen for laughter
Keen to be a dancer
Most days she'd be just like Prancer.

Her mother used to say,
'Nadine, why so keen?
Be nice, don't be mean.'

Taijarne Scott-Chandler (10)
St Mary's RC Primary School, Kilburn

A Naughty Boy

There was a naughty boy
And a naughty boy was he,
He ran away to Scotland
The people for to see,
There he found
That the ground
Was as hard,
That a yard
Was as long,
That a song
Was as merry,
That a cherry
Was as red,
That lead
Was as weighty,
That a fourscore
Was as eighty,
That a door
Was as wooden
As in England.
So he stood in his shoes
And he wondered,
He stood in his shoes
And he wondered.

Decio De Freitas (10)
St Mary's RC Primary School, Kilburn

Dogs

There are lots of different dogs around,
From little dogs to great big hounds.
Some like to jump and play in the park,
Some are quiet, but some like to bark.
I like to watch some dogs when they play,
But I love to watch my dog all day.

Ryan Jinadu (11)
St Mary's RC Primary School, Kilburn

Feelings

Monday I felt happy
Tuesday I felt sad
But why does nobody like me?
I haven't done anything bad.

Wednesday I felt angry
Thursday I felt embarrassed
I don't know why
But the class thought I was the shyest.
Friday I felt happy again
But it has already just begun.
Saturday I felt I had done something wrong
There were two bullies knocking on my door
And one of them said, 'Ping pong.'

Sunday I prayed
Then my dad died and I was sad
There my dad was in his grave he laid.

Gabriel Solomon (9)
St Mary's RC Primary School, Kilburn

Don't Judge A Book By Its Cover

Don't judge people by their size
Or the colour of their eyes
Don't tease people about their skin
Put all your insults in the bin
Make people happy, don't make them cry
Or their heart will die
Criticising is so cruel
Don't be mean, just play by the rules
It's rude to call someone skinny
Or say they have blubber
So in future
Please don't judge a book by its cover.

Sharon Ihemesinwa (10)
St Mary's RC Primary School, Kilburn

My Grandma Came From Switzerland

My grandma came from Switzerland,
She lived in the mountains on a farm.
She helped look after the animals
And kept them free from harm.
My grandma had a pet pig,
It was fat and round and pink,
She said her daddy roasted it
And left the tail in the sink.

Cameron Vaz (9)
St Mary's RC Primary School, Kilburn

Celebrations

R is for raspberry, yummy, yummy for my tummy
O is for orange, a sweet fruit
X is for X-ray for a broken bone
A is for apple, good for my tum, yum, yum, yum
N is for noodles, slippery, slimy
N is for nurse, to take care of me
E is for everyone to come to celebrate.

Roxanne Houston (9)
St Mary's RC Primary School, Kilburn

The Fish On The Dish

I need a fish on my dish and I don't know what to do.
I told the shoe mender I needed my shoe mended by half-past two.
He used a few glues on my shoe, but still it didn't look brand new.
I wished and I wished, I had a fish on my dish
And I don't know what to do.
I went on a big water slide, which was wild.
I was walking on a train track and eating a nice Big Mac.

Zalikha Harvey (9)
St Mary's RC Primary School, Kilburn

Bad Cooking

One day I made some sausages,
Then my mum came downstairs.
My mum said, 'Those don't look like sausages,
They are as hairy as bears.'

Another day I made a pancake,
Then my dad came downstairs.
He said, 'That looks like it has been burnt by flares.'

Then my sister came downstairs,
She ate a quarter of my pancake.
She would eat any burnt pancake. I don't think she cares.

Rhys Ambrose (11)
St Mary's RC Primary School, Kilburn

Cakes

Strawberry cakes,
Chocolate cakes,
Lemon cakes too,
They're all bad for you.
They make you feel funny,
Don't eat too many,
You might just turn into a *mummy.*

Tatiana Brazao (9)
St Mary's RC Primary School, Kilburn

Anger Poem

Volcanoes erupting with deadly, bad lava,
Heat burning up
And extreme bullets hitting you.
Tornadoes spinning everywhere.

Ivan Okpomor (8)
St Mary's RC Primary School, Kilburn

Sharks

I know a shark
His name is Mark,
He only comes out
When it is dark.

He's sleek and long
And likes eating tongues,
His teeth are like razors
And his eyes like lasers.

Michael Wiggins (10)
St Mary's RC Primary School, Kilburn

Voice Of An Angel

People say I've got the voice of an angel,
Others say I haven't.
There's tricky notes like la-la-la
And when I sing them
My brother says I sound like a sheep, baa, baa, baa.
When I sing funny,
All of my friends laugh, ha, ha, ha.
Now it's the end of my poem, bye, bye, bye,
I've got to fly, fly, fly.

Nancy Maguire (9)
St Mary's RC Primary School, Kilburn

Fun

Fun feels like the sun shining on your face
Fun looks like boys and girls playing bat and ball at the beach
Fun tastes like hot dogs at the park
Fun smells like doughnuts at the seaside
Fun sounds like clowns at the circus.

Daniel Makowski (7)
St Mary's RC Primary School, Kilburn

Delights

Cream cakes, cupcakes
I love all cakes
Cherries and cream
It's all a dream.
While I sleep
Memories creep
Of all delights
Through the night.
Blueberry muffins
And chocolate swirl
It makes me dribble.
My mum bakes fruit cakes
But make no mistake
I love chocolate cake!

Annabella Roberta (9)
St Mary's RC Primary School, Kilburn

My Poem About A Spider

I watched the little spider
Walk across the wall,
It dodged the picture frame
In the middle of the wall.

It walked up to the ceiling
And climbed the lumps of paint,
I saw lots of tiny footprints,
Although they were really faint.

The tiny little spider
Crawled up the chimney stack,
Avoided all the pitfalls,
But fell down a giant crack!

Christian Vaz (11)
St Mary's RC Primary School, Kilburn

Why?

Why am I alone all day?
Why do I cry all night and day?
Why don't I have any family and friends?
Why don't I have a doll to play with?
Why don't I have a brush to brush my hair?
Why don't I go to school to learn?
Why don't I have a mummy and daddy to care for me?
Why don't I have a brother and sister to play with me?
Why don't I have a book to read?
Why don't I have some jeans from Gap?
Why don't I have the things I have?
Because I am a little girl in a dustbin world.

Vivien da Silva (9)
St Mary's RC Primary School, Kilburn

A Happiness Poem

Happiness looks like a golden sun
Happiness sounds like some angels singing
Happiness feels like angels sleeping with you
Happiness tastes like God is inside you
Happiness smells like yellow daffodils.

Daniella Shakir (8)
St Mary's RC Primary School, Kilburn

The Morning Poem

I hate getting up in the morning
And going to school every day.
I'd rather stay and watch telly,
Or play my X-box all day.

Jamie O'Reilly (11)
St Mary's RC Primary School, Kilburn

In Wintertime

Snow as soft as sand,
A scarf as woolly as a pillow,
A snowball as hard as wood,
Heaters as hot as the sun,
Gloves as warm as a heater,
Hats as warm as a quilt,
A coat as long as a giraffe's neck.

Rebecca McCarthy (8)
St Mary's RC Primary School, Kilburn

Cold Winter Land

Snow as white as paper,
Snowballs as cold as snowmen,
Woolly hats as soft as a quilt,
Jumpers as blue as the sky,
Ice as cold as a freezer,
Scarves as long as a pipe,
Heaters as hot as the sun.

Dominique Odquier (8)
St Mary's RC Primary School, Kilburn

Amazing Winter

Snow as cold as ice,
Heaters as warm as an oven,
A scarf as long as a river,
A hat as woolly as a sheep,
Ice as fragile as glass,
A glove as warm as the sun.

Fatou Panzout (8)
St Mary's RC Primary School, Kilburn

Just Listen To Music

If you're in a bad mood, just listen to music,
If you're getting worked up, just listen to music.

If you wanna relax, just listen to music,
If you wanna chill, just listen to music.
You feel the vibe when you just listen to music,
You have the best thing of all, *fun,* when you
Just listen to music!

Courtnee Haley (10)
St Mary's RC Primary School, Kilburn

Winter Wonderland

A jumper as woolly as a sheep,
A heater as warm as the sun,
A scarf as long as a tree,
A snowball as round as a ball,
Ice as cold as snow,
Ice skates as sharp as a needle,
Snow as cold as Iceland.

Jessica Ofodile (8)
St Mary's RC Primary School, Kilburn

Snow Fun

Ice as fragile as china,
Snowball as hard as ice,
Snow is cold as a freezer,
Ice skates as sharp as a blade,
A scarf as long as a ladder,
Gloves as warm as a cat.

Dakota Manser (8)
St Mary's RC Primary School, Kilburn

The Tragic Boxing Day

The day was done,
Christmas was fun.
Our friends had to hurry away,
The lights on the tree
Were lovely to see,
But tomorrow was another day.

It was just after one,
When I noticed the sun
Was hiding behind a grey cloud.
Suddenly much noise
Came from little boys,
'The sea's coming fast and loud.'

The ocean rose high,
It reached for the sky,
Smashing the boats in its path.
We ran and we fell,
It was really like Hell,
Who knows what caused so much wrath.

Whenever I see,
The vast, cruel sea,
It will always fill me with dread.
That terrible day,
When life flickered away
And left so many souls dead.

Andrea Fernando (10)
St Mary's RC Primary School, Kilburn

A Happiness Poem

Happiness looks like golden sand
Happiness feels like angels floating around
Happiness tastes like a picnic on a hill
Happiness smells like a white rose
Happiness sounds like birds singing.

Jessica Rosario-Brown
St Mary's RC Primary School, Kilburn

Me

My name is *Mark*,
I like playing in the park.

I'm eleven years old,
And sometimes bold!

Paul is my brother,
Michelle my sister.

Tracy is my mother,
Derek my dad.

Mark Lacey (11)
St Mary's RC Primary School, Kilburn

Friends

I love to play with my friends
I hate it when the fun ends.
I love to play in the sun
And the rain and having fun.
I feel so sad when we have a fight.
I feel so angry all night.
When you find a good friend,
Make sure your friendship never ends.

Lawrence Dunn (10)
St Mary's RC Primary School, Kilburn

Fear

Fear looks like a bloodthirsty tiger
Fear smells like a snake's breath
Fear feels like hanging off a building
Fear tastes like spider stew
Fear sounds like a howling wolf.

Christy Conor Haynes (8)
St Mary's RC Primary School, Kilburn

My Brother's Fart Machine

My brother has a fart machine,
That's kinda like a tube
But when you blow into it,
Out comes something rude.

My brother has a fart machine,
Which has never really smelt
Cos all it is is a toilet tube
Wrapped round in blue felt.

One day my brother's fart machine,
Was found lying in the bin.
Later we discovered that,
Mum had put it in.

My brother saved his fart machine,
From its destiny in there
And now you still hear farting sounds,
Floating through the air.

Joshua Haynes-Mannering (10)
St Mary's RC Primary School, Kilburn

A Game

Game 1:   This is going to be fun
Game 2:   I am going to get you
Game 3:   You're coming to get me
Game 4:   I will knock at your door
Game 5:   I am at your house
Game 6:   You beat me with sticks
Game 7:   I go to Heaven
Game 8:   I meet a mate
Game 9:   He asks me if I am fine
Game 10:   I ask if I can have another go again.

Daniel Martins (11)
St Mary's RC Primary School, Kilburn

Summertime

Flowers so bright, grass so green,
Summer is here, I love the sun,
We swim in the sea, we walk in the sand.

It's holiday time I feel so grand,
We've had so much fun.
Now we must run
To look at the sunset before we forget.

Tara Quinn (10)
St Mary's RC Primary School, Kilburn

Nosebleed

I had a nosebleed,
It bled all day long,
It bleeds all over my books,
I don't know why it bleeds so much.

Ben Dodge (11)
St Mary's RC Primary School, Kilburn

Listen

Listen to the sound of the music.
The drums, the beat,
You will never get tired
If you listen to the sound of the
         Music.

Nadia Andrew (10)
St Mary's RC Primary School, Kilburn

Being Happy

I like being happy,
When there's no school.
I like being happy
When I'm cool.

I like being happy
When it's my birthday.
I like being happy when
I'm going on a holiday.

I like being happy
When it's Christmas day
I like being happy when
It's New Year's day!

Jade Warner-Clayton (10)
St Mary's RC Primary School, Kilburn

The Wind Is Angry And Sad

The wind is angry
It pounds on the door
Shouts and weeps
Slumps off with a roar.

The wind is sorry
It smoothes out the sky
Whispers and creeps
While the birds try to fly.

The wind is happy
The wind is sad
The wind is angry
The wind is mad.

Jake O'Neill (9)
St Mary's RC Primary School, Kilburn

The Magic Box

(Based on 'Magic Box' by Kit Wright)

I will put in my box . . .

The moment I opened my eyes and saw my parents,
Happy moments with my cousin,
The smell of my mam in her favourite perfume.

I will put in my box . . .

My first bubble bath,
The sound of happiness,
The smell of my mum's cooking.

I will put in my box . . .

The taste of McDonald's,
The moment I saw my favourite singer,
The smell of my grandmother.

I will put in my box . . .

The moment when Dad kisses me a goodnight kiss,
The moment I spent in school.
The moonlight from my bedroom window.

I will put in my box . . .

The first time I ate the moon, it is like cheese,
And jumped from the hill to see my sister in the stars.

My box is fashioned from gold to glitter
With hearts on the lid and stories on the bottom
And laughs in the corner.

I shall play in my box all day long
And have a swim in the wild sea
And be a happy person all the day.

Hadab Al-Homayed (10)
The Hampshire School

My Magic Box

(Based on 'Magic Box' by Kit Wright)

I will put in my box . . .

The way dogs lick,
The smell of cut grass,
The sound of robins singing.

I will put in my box . . .

The first time I sang,
The first moment I spoke,
The first time I lost a tooth.

I will put in my box . . .

The day of my birth,
The first time I opened my eyes,
The first time someone hugged me.

I will put in my box . . .

The bluest piece of ocean,
The sunset over a beach,
The fish that tickle my toe.

My box lid has a ruby handle,
A range of silver hinges,
And is covered with thoughts.

I will sleep in my box,
All my dreams will escape,
All my thoughts will come back,
My heart will open
To a world I don't know.

Alix Regnier (9)
The Hampshire School

My Magic Box

(Based on 'Magic Box' by Kit Wright)

I will put in my box . . .

The sunrise in Africa,
Seaside waves of Sicily,
Magic red hot ground of a safari.

I will put in my box . . .

Angry waves crashing on rocks,
Joyful sweet song of winter robins,
Gentle sound of a snowflake smashing.

I will put in my box . . .

Lots of joy from my heart,
Caring love of my parents,
The magical gift of light.

I will put in my box . . .

The fresh smell of my love,
The confident smell of friendship,
The lovely smell of fresh bread.

My box has topaz corners,
A wooden lid
And silver sides and bottom.

I shall run quickly,
I will swim the seven seas,
Then I shall climb the highest mountain.
After, I will love who gave me life.
Finally I shall rest in peace forever.

Giuliano Federico Ricciardi (10)
The Hampshire School

Dragon And Cat

(Based on 'The Owl and the Pussycat' by Edward Lear)

Dragon and Cat lived together
On a cloud with fifty-five rooms.
Dragon owned bats and Cat hats,
And ate rice and mice,
Until they got bored.
Cat shouted, 'I want something new.'
'Me too.'
And they went on a journey around the world.
They looked,
They looked,
Looked,
Looked.

'This is fun!' said the cat
'I feel sick!' answered her friend.
'You have been eating too much food!' said Cat,
and then they played with a ball and a bat.
'I feel better now,' Dragon said.
'Look! There is a crazy cow with a hat!'

They landed in China and went to buy a few things.
Cat bought Nutella and Dragon toast.

They got back to the cloud and Dragon fried toast,
And Cat spread Nutella.
And they have been eating it from that day on!

Erika Koljonen (10)
The Hampshire School

The Monkey And The Zebra

(Based on 'The Owl and the Pussycat' by Edward Lear)

The monkey and the zebra went away
They went to the North Pole,
Then zebra said, 'Let us go on a bike,'
So they set off to make their goal.

They took with them many a thing
They took with them jam and toast,
A tent and a football toilet brush,
And a chicken they planned to roast.

They took their wills and cooked their shills
And they made an igloo for two.
They went sledding all day until they met
A polar bear they already knew.

The bear was a priest which was most fortunate,
And the zebra and monkey married indeed
The zebra said, 'Please be my bride.'
They saw a ring on the polar bear's head and they
Married indeed.

The beautiful ring was made out of ice
And all of two days after
It got very hot and the ring didn't last
The monkey had cried but the zebra had laughter.

Aliya Dewey (9)
The Hampshire School

The Ant And The Blue Whale

(Based on 'The Owl and the Pussycat' by Edward Lear)

The ant and the blue whale went to Saturn's ring,
Flying on a dog's big fat wing,
When the ant said, 'How sweetly you sing,
You sing,
You sing.'

When they got to the ring,
They saw a basketball and the whale said,
'Why don't we play,
We play,
We play,
Good fellow small?'

Then the ant said, 'Because you're too tall,
Too tall,
Too tall,
And I'm only small.'

The whale remembered those words that the ant said
On the wing,
The wing,
The wing,
So he then began to sing,
'Man you is da best, it is da unbeatable team,
Da team,
Da team'
And the ant interrupted, 'You got that superly - duperly wrong,
Cos I hate that song,
That song,
That song.'

When the whale shouted in full volume,
'We will now finally go to Planet Football,
Football,
Football!

So off they went,
Now on a butterfly's wing.
When they got there, they saw Arsenal's football pitch,
So off they jolly well went to see Arsenal v Manchester United.
The match was infinite, so they rested in peace,
In peace,
In peace.
(They are still watching the football match right now!)

Francisco Botelho (9)
The Hampshire School

The Mosquito And The Leopard
(Based on 'The Owl and the Pussycat' by Edward Lear)

The mosquito and the leopard got on a plane
They flew and they flew until they reached Spain.
Their passports got rejected, they couldn't stay,
So they got back on their plane, and flew to Bombay.

They there bought some cheese and several pet bees
To use for fun when they fly.

'Oh!' said the leopard, 'Married we should be!'
'Hey!' said the mosquito, 'Propose to me!'
'Very well,' said the leopard, 'Propose I shall,'
He put the plane on autopilot, and knelt with a bow.

'There is only one problem' said the leopard, said he.
'I've no ring, and worse no money.'
'Now don't you blame me you spotty ol' thing,
when we first went out I thought it was just a fling!'

'Whatever! Don't fuss! We'll find something.'
He then made a daisy chain to use as a ring.

'At last we'll be married,' said the leopard, said he
'Now give us a kiss, you stunning mozzie.'

Jessika Anne Faithfull (10)
The Hampshire School

My Magic Box

(Based on 'Magic Box' by Kit Wright)

I will put in my box . . .

The feeling of water splashing on my face,
The sight of Florida sunshine,
The laughter of my family enjoying themselves.

I will put in my box . . .

A hamster having a sip of apple cider,
A taste of a hot dog burning on my tongue,
A cow jumping over the moon.

I will put in my box . . .

The Eiffel Tower, all seven of them!
A butterfly on a horse!
And a cowboy flying across the field.

My box will be glazed with happiness
With the smell of violets,
My future of joy.

I sing in my box
In a great enormous band
Of the Sun's everlasting island
Then swish away to the mountains
With my magic box!

Nosa Omosigho (10)
The Hampshire School

My Best Friend

My best friend,
Is the best friend I know
Nothing is the same without my best friend
She's got blonde hair that shines like the sun
She's got red, juicy lips
That shine every time I come near her
She has rosy cheeks
That is as red, as a rose
She's got a pierced nose that sparkles in the night
Her teeth are as white as snow
She wears blue fashion jeans and a pink shirt
She is just like my girlfriend
She's got blue eyes, that look like the clear, blue ocean
We always do things together
Sometimes we go to the cinema
She wears a bandana when we go out
I think she wears it to show off
I cannot forget the day it snowed
We would have been best friends forever
We always do wordsearch competitions
Sometimes I win
Sometimes she does
Every Sunday we go skateboarding
Sometimes we have to cancel it
Because we have to go to birthday parties
Her best game is bowling
Mine too
We sometimes listen to music
Our favourite singer is Mario
Our favourite song is Baby Let Me Love You
We sometimes go ice skating
We always go there in the winter
And when we have school days off
I hope our friendship would last for a long time.

Lucas Trattou (10)
West Green JMI School

Emotions And Beliefs

I feel like a wild antelope,
Charging through all I can.
I feel like a ferocious bear,
Destroying everything in my path.
I feel like a cat,
Brave and willing to explore the road ahead.

I feel like a dog,
Courageous and loyal.
I feel like an elephant,
Big and important.
I feel like a fish,
Showing off as much as I can.

I feel like a giraffe
With my tall neck, reaching above the clouds.
I feel like a horse,
Racing and always in competition.
I feel like an insect,
Puny and inferior to others.

I feel like a jellyfish,
Always protected from all others.
I feel like a kangaroo,
Jumping over every obstacle that I come across
I feel like a lion,
Fierce and indestructible.

I have lots of emotions
And feelings.
But as long as my
Friends and family
Are always there to support me,
The one thing I will never feel is to be,
Alone.

Daniel Harris (11)
West Green JMI School

A Zookeeper In The Zoo

A zookeeper in the zoo
Would see the tall giraffes,
Reaching out for the leaves,
On the tallest luscious trees.
A zookeeper in the zoo
Would hear the thudding trotting
Of the elephant's heavy feet,
As if marching into battle.
A zookeeper in the zoo,
Would taste ripe bananas,
From the banana trees.
A zookeeper in the zoo,
Would hope for the fierce rhinos,
Not to attack him.
A zookeeper in a zoo,
Would feel the soft fur stresses,
Of the lion's mane.
A zookeeper in a zoo,
Would smell the beautiful
Fresh scent of the exotic orchids.

A zookeeper in the zoo,
Would feed the chimpanzees,
And swim in the deep green lake,
With the large enormous hippos.

A zookeeper in the zoo,
Would hear the screaming,
Of the deer being eaten
By the vicious cheetahs.

Radha Wahyuwidayat (8)
West Green JMI School

When I'm With My Family

When I'm with my family I can see butterflies,
Fluttering by me,
I can see flowers growing around me,
Beautiful and stunning.

When I'm with my family, I feel the tree of life,
Growing inside me,
I can feel birds flying around in my stomach,
I can feel the wind in my hair.

When I'm with my family, I can hear laughter,
Birds chirping and music ringing in my ears,
I can hear harp's melodic sound.

When I'm with my family, I can taste strawberries
And cream on my tongue.
I can taste ice cream melting in my mouth.

When I'm with my family, I can smell perfume,
The fresh smell permeating into the air.
I can smell herbs and mint,
Wafting up my nose.
I can smell the sweetness of honey and the smell
Of my mum's cooking.

When I'm with my family, I hope for love and cherish
The future to come.
I hope for kindness and my family to grow bigger
And so do our hearts grow bigger,
And probably we'll never know, my family could be
Part of history, of something special indeed.

When I'm with my family, I dream of one day
We can be the Royal Family.

Esra Mansour
West Green JMI School

The Aborigines Of Australia

Trees with their leaves swaying side to side,
Like a bird flying through the air.
Kangaroos jumping like the fireworks jumping jacks.
As the lively day goes on
The minutes turn into hours
The shining sun like a devil's lair
Burning, boiling, scolding
Now it was hotter than the centre of the Earth.

Now jumping and dancing on the sand
Other people playing instruments.
Lizards swaying fast in the sand like shooting rockets.
The crocodile grinning with his white knife-like teeth at his prey.
All now running away.
But the people still dance on
Into the Australian desert night.

Edward Hacking (9)
Westminster Cathedral Choir School

Aborigines Of Australia

The Aborigines dancing in the blazing flame.
A kangaroo joining in with her young in her pouch.
The anteater with its tongue like a spiro.
The fish flying through the water like a colourful bullet.
The water like purple velvet.
The crocodile's scales shimmering in the light like a silver moon
Its teeth shining like stars.
The colourful bird showing off its meticulous feathers,
While eating berries off the mountwicker tree.
The trees leaves like brown beady eyes.
The snake slithering underground like a worm going through a book.
The fire bursting out blood-red like a volcano.
The colours like a multicoloured rainbow.
The scorching flame dying away by the velvet water.

James Machin (9)
Westminster Cathedral Choir School

Fireworks Poem

Fireworks, fireworks, fireworks
Every year, new wonders
Flaming Roman candles and
Spinning Catherine wheels
Rockets that shatter into a shower of sapphires
Emerald stars and golden rain
Glistening in the deep blue sky
Brilliant bangs and blazing booms
Like the Earth exploding.
The night is magnificent, the fireworks fade.

Lawrence Speaight (8)
Westminster Cathedral Choir School

The Wish Of The Kite

I am a kite, I love windy weather
I toss and I turn, swoop, and I glide
While steadily streaking through the air
The wind is beating on my canvas
I swish and I swoosh
I wish it would go on forever and ever
With the wind howling, whistling, screeching
I somersault like a gymnast
I dive like a hawk
I sail like a ship in full wind.

Philippe Marchant (9)
Westminster Cathedral Choir School

White Tigers - Haiku

White tigers running
With their black stripes on their back.
Plain white teeth for claws.

Jasper Ford-Welman (9)
Westminster Cathedral Choir School

The Wish Of The Frog

My name is Fabulous Freddie,
(I have a brother - his name is Teddy)
We both enjoy splashing around
In our pond, in the middle of town.

Today is dreary, wet and cold
But we don't care because we're bold.
We love the drizzle, the storms and rain
For other folk, it can be a pain.

But not for us; this is our home
Of floating leaves and no telephone.
We swim all day, or sometimes just float
We are so agile, no need for a boat.

You see we only care when it rains
Because without any water, it is just not the same
We will only dry out a - a shame, a pity,
And the pond becomes muddy - and that's really sticky.

Now evening is coming and we need some sleep.
Our heads hit the water and we sleep like Bo-Peep.
We wrap ourselves in our watery bed
And sleep the sleep of the nearly, just dead.

Christopher Short (8)
Westminster Cathedral Choir School

Fireworks

Big, green fireworks upon the dark sky above the sun.
Away from all of us, high, high, in the sky.
The golden sun shines like a firework.
It blasted into the air like a bouncing bat.
It will spin like a golden globe, then explode into a screaming
Riot then it falls into showers.
'What an amazing sight!'
I blasted another one into the sky,
Upon the golden moon with a flaming red explosion.

Alasdair Grassie (9)
Westminster Cathedral Choir School

Winter Days

Shimmering days
Snowy Earth
Glittering snow
Like crystals.

Frosty wind
Thrashing over
The cold
Happy people.

Snowing hard
Nice and crispy
A sparkling duvet
Covers the world.

An avalanche of snowflakes
Hail, bitter snows
Drifts into the trees.

The snowflakes dancing down
Like little meringues!

Ferdinand Rex (8)
Westminster Cathedral Choir School

The Wish Of A Flytrap

I wish there were more flies around
So I can eat
The taste of the body
The crunch of the wings
Make my mouth water.
I'll open my mouth for a landing stage
I spread my succulent petals
I get that tingling feeling
Then *snap!*
I've got my dinner.

Oliver Swan (9)
Westminster Cathedral Choir School

Every Reindeer Herders Of Siberia

Moonlight shining like gold,
Shimmering in the sky
A reindeer like a shadow,
Reminding me of St Nicholas.
A tree as tall as Mount Everest twinkling in the moonlight
Clouds like mountains, snow-topped
That reminded me of Chamonix.
Two Eskimos riding a sleigh so high in the sky
Maroon trees so huge
Towering like a giant, looking down on everything.
The night is pitch-black only with the moon to light it up.
Stars twinkling so brightly, so high.
Two birds flying at night.
Two sleeping Eskimos on a reindeer flying so high
With the stars shimmering in the moonlight.
Two birds, as quiet as a mouse eating beige leaves
Which had a blood red trunk.
Church towers peeping out of a hill like witches' fingers.
A sleigh jingling off in the moonlight.

George Mitchell (9)
Westminster Cathedral Choir School

Disappearing Worlds

A man holding a harpoon as sharp as a dagger.
Skin like a bark of a tree.
A skirt as red as the sun and as yellow as a banana too.
Leaves cling to his arms and waist like short palm leaves.
Trees as green as their leaves.
Exotic birds flying through the sky, like twinkling stars in space.
Three huts made of straw, but one is oh so green.
A snake silently slithers slyly across the ground.
A bird looking for grub.
A man holding a pig.
Skirt so yellow and carpety skin.
Birds have tails twirling like mad. Wow!

Oliver Togias-Howells (8)
Westminster Cathedral Choir School

Wanted, A Dragon

Wanted, a dragon
Able to fly,
Can breathe fire
Master of the sky.

Wanted, a dragon,
Smooth or rough,
Whichever you see
Has to be tough.

Wanted, a dragon
With very good ears,
And teeth and claws
As sharp as spears.

Wanted, a dragon
As quick as a lizard,
That never obeys anyone
Except his owner wizard.

Wanted, a dragon
With pointy ears
When he flies
Over town everyone fears.

Wanted, a dragon
With wings like a plane,
That turns quickly in the air
Like a huge weathervane.

Nicholas Eterovic (8)
Westminster Cathedral Choir School

Cheetah

Teeth like needles,
Fur like golden flames,
Speed like fire,
Dancing on the spot.

Theo Bakker (8)
Westminster Cathedral Choir School

The Wish Of The Cold

I hope that the weather always stays cold,
So the human defences are weakened,
We want to cause miserable people,
And take control of the body like nerves alerting the brains.
We wish to dodge the mucus,
To laugh at the rising heat,
We wish to massacre the white blood cells,
To make the eyes water and weep,
We wish for the body to lie down,
For us to turn worse and worse,
For us to gradually change,
We wish for the body to writhe in its sleep,
For us to spread like fungi,
And for us to change from worse to worse to
Flu!

Julian Hartley (8)
Westminster Cathedral Choir School

Firework Poem!

Green dragons rise from the ground,
Like olives popping.
A Roman candle rises high like sprouting vegetables.

A red whirling Catherine wheel goes up into the air,
Out up into the night sky,
A navy blue gowned flower – explodes high.

A big, bang, loudly came down and disappeared from sight.
A quick Nighthawk missile zooms through the night sky
Like a fighter jet rocket.

A turquoise sparrow missile
Shoots across the sky and bursts in mid-air
A military missile almost towers the sky
Like a space rocket.

Luke Olver (8)
Westminster Cathedral Choir School

The Brazilian Rainforest

The emerald trees gleaming like diamonds
With purple, maroon, turquoise and magenta parrots
Gliding through the sapphire sky.
The clear blue river sparkles with turtles, dolphins and
Frogs zooming through the ultra-marine water.
The tribesmen hunt with silver sharp arrows and wooden bows.
The yellow happy cheetah staring at the topaz monkey
Eating an amber banana.
While all this time, three tribesmen sleep in ebony hammocks.
All the women searching for lime, apple and melon.
The amethyst rainforest is full of colour.

Barnaby Lynch (8)
Westminster Cathedral Choir School

Firework Poem

Bouncing bats explode like fiery flowers
Tumbling demons glance at the moonlight
Galactic granite inspires the stars
Super space rockets zoom past the night sky.

Fantastic fish are fountains of fire
Zooming zebras explode in black and white
Dancing dogs spray light in the air
Noisy newts mutate into blown up bulls.

Roland Abbott (8)
Westminster Cathedral Choir School

Water-Cats - Haiku

Water-cat swimming
He is blue and black blazing
Water-cat is you!

Charles Ingell (8)
Westminster Cathedral Choir School

The African Tribe

Deep in the dense, African jungle is a chief of a tribe,
Brandishing a harpoon, as sharp as the sharpest knife.

An emerald and golden-yellow Maliwa-snake slithers
Across the peaty ground.

Clonkerjonkerbilious trees rise from the ground
Like giant sea anemones.

An emu-like mahogany coloured bird struts along as if he
Is the king of the jungle.

A man holds a piglet whilst herding pigs, cocks and hens.

Birds with feathers of incarnardine, cream, off-white, ecru,
Gold, amber and khaki sit with exotic tails, including a mauve
And lilac cockatoo,
Magenta and cerise crest on his head with its scarlet, amber
And vermilion spouse.

A dog drinks out of a bucket, just outside the farmyard,
Whilst a hedgehog curls up like a thorn bush.

Edward Hackett (8)
Westminster Cathedral Choir School

Fireworks Poem

They scream across the starry sky,
Roaring rockets raging, red and ruby,
Light the air with shimmering stars,
Of ochre, turquoise and green.

Sparkling spirits spin across the ground,
Glowing sapphire demons,
Erupt into enormous showers of emerald
Until they disappear into the night.

Fantastic fizzing fairies, frolic above our heads,
Exploding in amazing bursts of diamond lighting,
Finally it's over and the fireworks are gone,
And all we have are fantasies, to take us to our beds.

Charlie Davies (8)
Westminster Cathedral Choir School

The Fantastic Door

(Inspired by 'The Door' by Miroslav Holub)

Go and open the door
Maybe outside there's
A silk sky
Or a wood with pixies and enchantments.

Go and open the door
Maybe there's a forest with wizards and witches
Or a tiger or a lion.

Go and open the door
Maybe there's a star twinkling in the sky
Or a dog dancing in the sky.

Peter Burke-Smith (8)
Westminster Cathedral Choir School

The Chewing Gum

Rubber, rubber chewing gum
You can chew it up and down
Elastic gum that lasts all day
Don't even bother to bend and pray!

Super, duper, chewing gum
You can bend it up and down
Twist it in curly knots
50p that's all it costs!

Chewy, gooey chewing gum
Elastic rubber you chew around
When you go to bed and pray
Buy it at the shop the next day!

Kamil Sekerali (10)
Whitmore Primary School

Look At The Sea

Look at the sea going up and down
Look at the sea going round and round
Look at the waves clashing together.
Look at the colours white . . . blue . . . and green
All different colours nice calm sea
Is that what you want? Maybe.
Up and down round and round
Imagine the birds flying on top of us
Singing a beautiful song.
Just imagine the sea for you and me.

Nathifa Dawkins-Alexander (11)
Whitmore Primary School

Troublemaker

Troublemaker, troublemaker
Knock the door troublemaker
Troublemaker break the floor
Troublemaker, troublemaker
Break the glass troublemaker
Troublemaker run so fast
Troublemaker, troublemaker
Say you're sorry troublemaker
Troublemaker you're very lucky.

Tyrelle Glasgow (11)
Whitmore Primary School

My Own Playground Poem

The playground blushes as a light bulb switching off.
The sky is white, like snow coming down.
The sound of a motorbike sounds like a tiger, rough.
The grass looks as green, as green grass in the playground.

Alex Demetriou (8)
Whitmore Primary School

Mother Kennings

TV watcher
Food cooker
House cleaner
Gameboy player
Chair sitter
Happy maker
Job finder
Bedroom cleaner
Song writer
Babysitter
Homework writer
Basketball player
Sports player
Shopaholic
Teacher teacher
Cake maker
Ice cream maker
Chef cooker
Mother lady
Mother lover
Super Mum
Children maker
Argument stopper
Strong woman
This is the best Mother in the world
This is Dami's mum's poem.

Dami Jinadu (10)
Whitmore Primary School

Playground In The Cold

Leaves crunching under your feet.
The grass, green as peas.
The sun is hiding behind the clouds.
The leaves are as brown as a brown stick.
The sky is as grey as smoke out of a chimney.

Precious Omorogbe (8)
Whitmore Primary School

Brother Kennings

TV watcher
Game player
Team player
TV turn offer
Football fan
Fighter
Sport fan
PS2 player
Bad liar
Slow walker, fast walker.

Mehmet Gerekli (9)
Whitmore Primary School

Foggy Day

In the foggy day, you can't see anything in the dark misty day.
The fog is like the smoke from a fire.
The aeroplane zooms through the fog, like after its lunch.
The wind blows like a waving fan.
The clouds are covering the sun like bodyguards.
The cars go past as the fog carries on.
The leaves are rustling like maracas underfoot.

Anh Pham (9)
Whitmore Primary School

The Lightning Power

The sky gloomy like lead.
The lightning is like, it's throwing pencils in your eyes.
Heaven is like crashing like the Titanic, hitting an iceberg.
The injured people are like a wild beast in his chains.
It fell, like you're being crunched by a lion, that hasn't had its lunch
It sounds like a beast roaring.

Jay Fenton (8)
Whitmore Primary School

Christmas Time

It is Christmas, bells ringing, everyone out in the snow
Making a snowman throwing snowballs
Sing-a-longs to Christmas songs in the cold, all day long.

Buy presents, put them under the great big tree
Dress the tree with a big great star
Wonderful shopping, the tree is green, you can see things
Like hollies and other decorations.

You get up, with joy, sprint to your presents,
See all your fantastic things
Go to Christmas dinner with your family
Eat pudding!

Nicole Ansell (10)
Whitmore Primary School

Playground In Water

Out in the playground birds sound as happy as clowns,
Feet stomping like horses running.
Mud as soft as a teddy bear, slippery as ice
Leaves as crunchy as bones breaking
And bushes as spiky as swords.
The sky is as dark as a shadow on the floor
And cars sound as loud as a bulldozer.

Kaya Fedai (9)
Whitmore Primary School

The Playground Noise

The football players, play football as loud as builders.
The children run like horses.
The teachers shout like pigs.
The teachers blow their whistle, how pigs oink.
The wind blows through the trees and the trees rattle.

Tashana Destouche (8)
Whitmore Primary School

Embarrassing Mum!

My mum is very embarrassing.
She embarrasses me in front of the public every single day.
She shouts hello, when I'm on the phone,
So my friend can hear that she's there.
She calls out my foot size in the clothes shop.
She kisses her boyfriend in public and she even wears my miniskirt
When she's going out.

Everyone in the street knows that she's very embarrassing,
But I just wish she'd stop embarrassing me in public.

Flore Kadianga (10)
Whitmore Primary School

Hackney

Hackney is a brilliant place,
If you see it's better than a smiley face.
If you drive near Hackney you should come and see.
It will be fun for you and will be fun for me.

There's libraries, museums and houses too.
If you want to get a job you'll surely get through.

Everywhere you go, you won't see any litter,
Every place is sweeter than a Banana fritter!

Farren Cummings (10)
Whitmore Primary School

School Poem's Not To Be Missed

The clouds are grey as if they have been painted.
The wood cracks like fireworks have been let off.
Concrete is slippery as a worm
The leaves thin, like soft paper.
The mud smells like it's wet sand.

Sevgi Firat (9)
Whitmore Primary School

School Poems

The robin is blushing to burn his face to death just like a sun.

The playground is calm, playful but dangerous when the
lightning strikes.
The playground flashes like a wasted light bulb.

Out in the playground, you might see some rain and
Inside you're just a big bad pain.

Inside the lunch hall you might see some rubbish,
But at least you're eating a big bag of cabbage.

Outside the playground you skip, hop, jump and run
And you might even crawl like a tiny spider.

Kevin Voang (9)
Whitmore Primary School

Out In The Playground

In the playground, the birds sound as happy as a clown,
They echo as loud as animals' feet.

There's mud under my feet as soft as a cushion.

Concrete as hard as metal, climbing frames
Floor as soggy as wet paper.
The sky is as dark as a shadow and moves as slow as a snail.

Shae Oram (8)
Whitmore Primary School

Snow

Snow looks white as the sky
Ice is slippery as a slippery rock
Snow feels cold and wet
Ice when you swish it, it makes a cranky noise
Snow smells normal.

Dina Sammut (9)
Whitmore Primary School

Nature

As I step, I hear the leaves crunch like sweet wrappers.
As the wind blows, the trees start to swing their branches around.
The birds sing so sweet as a Christmas carol.
Crows communicate with each other,
Telling about fat, juicy, slimy, sticky worms.
The moon is so bright, brighter than a silver ring.

Anna Oluwalana (8)
Whitmore Primary School

The Bees Chorus

(Based on 'The Pelican Chorus' by Edward Lear)

King and Queen of bees are we
Yellow and black lines go across me.
We are the best small creatures of them all
We have some honey then we start to play ball.
Breskin broski brakskin Bill
We thought so then and we think so still.

We live in grass, we live on pollen
We had a son and we named him Colin.
We fly around, we think of something
When someone gets mean to us, we give them a sting.
Breskin broskin brakskin Bill
We thought so then and we think so still.

We're not that big, we're not that fat
We're just the right size and we're scared of a cat.
We are the smartest we earn our lives
Did you know we live in hives?
Breskin broskin brakskin Bill
We thought so then, we think so still.

Anthony Mba (9)
Wyvil Primary School

The Spiders' Chorus

(Based on 'The Pelican Chorus' by Edward Lear)

Duke and duchess of the spiders we
No other creature so fond as we
None have feet like sticks
With lovely hairy body and bits.

Stunkskin, stankskin spiders' tree
No other creature so powerful as we
Stickskin, stackskin, spider bill
We thought so then and we thought to kill.

We live in the tree, the tree we love
By night we sleep on the hills above
By day we hunt for precious food
Which gets us in a very good mood
At eve we stand on the hot yellow sand
Which gets us banned from our very own land.

Jumpskin, jempskin, spider's back
Red and white and darkest black
Jampskin, jumpsuit, spiders dead
They lay on their little tiny bed.

Gustavo Hondrato (10)
Wyvil Primary School

Future

The colours of my future are beautiful.
Yellow and orange it is.
It reminds me of my family,
We are beautiful, handsome and full of harmony.
It sounds like peaceful music, Mozart, Chopin, Mendelssohn too.
It tastes like vanilla ice cream, yum, yum, yummy.
It smells like healthy air, God provided everywhere.
It looks like my future.
A judge on the high bench.

Segun Soji-Akingboye (10)
Wyvil Primary School

Songbird Of The Silver Screen

I want to be a good singer
And perform on the stage
Wear beautiful gowns and lipstick,
And be on the front page.
I'd like to meet popstars, famous ones too
If I could sing, I'll meet my fans
Well, it depends on who.
You know I'll wear my blings.
I want to be the best singer
And be proud of myself
Be a famous singer, make new friends
I'll sing out loud, see friends
I'd like to sing for royalty,
And be paid handsomely too.

Adaeze Ugochukwu (9)
Wyvil Primary School

Happiness And Love

Happiness is like listening to my Mariah Kerry CD.
Happiness is the bubbling of lemonade in my mouth.
Happiness is like the sweet taste of cherryade in the afternoon.
When I'm happy it feels like I've been to Heaven and back.

Love is like a newborn baby
Love is like a laughter of two lovers
Love is like a kiss on my head and
A hug from Grandmom and Grandfather
When I'm unhappy my mum and dad call me over
With a kiss on the head and a really long hug.

Latifaha Ireland (10)
Wyvil Primary School

I Remember

I remember the day
I moved away,
I was so sad
My mum couldn't make me glad.
Then I saw my sister Rose
She was changing her clothes,
She was so happy she got snappy.
My baby brother was changing his nappy.
The only thing that could make me happy
Was if my grandpa brought my swan Floppy,
But now he's dead
I had to change my name to Fred.
He was my life,
He got me through everything,
When I was down,
He brought me up,
And never flopped.
When I was two
I had the 'flu'
He made me soup,
And I felt better.
Now it's time to say goodbye
To all my friends and they cry,
But it's time to go
And I know it's hard for you,
But I give a mere reflection of me on a picture,
Please don't cry,
I had to sigh,
I tried to keep my tears inside.

Emmanuel Oguntimirin (10)
Wyvil Primary School

Life

Life is a ring to a bell,
The spark in my eye,
A robin flying by.
The words of a song,
The right not the wrong,
The fish in the sea,
The busy old bee.
The Moon and Sun
The flowers that sprung,
The wind in my ear,
The gloss in my hair.
A song from my heart,
A kiss in the dark,
A hug from my mum,
When I'm feeling glum.
A hum in my head.
A cosy old bed.
A wish in the night,
The sun shining bright.
An everlasting dream.
A long winding stream.

Le-Reisse Douglas (10)
Wyvil Primary School

Sunflower

Sunflower, sunflower, my yellow sunflower
My sunflower has got lots of power
Shushing through the wind,
You sing, you pray
I'm speechless, there's nothing I can say.
I've told you this,
You're beautiful in a very special way.

Sofia Cabral (10)
Wyvil Primary School

Amusement

Amusement is as blue as the morning sky
With birds, skylarks and pigeons flying by.
It's like happiness and laughter
In the dark sky after.

It sounds like a laughing bear
Which laughs so much it floats in the air.
Amusement smells like a rose
When its petals close.

It also looks like smiley faces
In all its different places.
Amusement feels like you've got laughing gas on you
Wash it off and you'll get better too!

Amusement tastes like a sweet tangerine
That is lovely, juicy and ever so clean
It reminds me of water
When I go to the king's house to crack jokes
With his daughter.

Abigail Ashmead (9)
Wyvil Primary School

Dance

Dance, dance music to my feet
It makes me feel like a queen
I dance all night, I dance all day
I feel my heart beating
Bang, bang hey
I click my fingers
And I tap my feet
I click my whole body like the sea
My mother asked me why do I dance so much?
I say I just can't resist.

Alfredtina Boaitey (10)
Wyvil Primary School

Love

Love is red and reminds me of a rose,
A kiss from my nan on top of my nose.
Love is calm, smells like flowers too
But love really reminds me of you.

Love tastes like lemon flavour ice cream
Eating on my bed
But while you're at it put a fruit in,
Strawberries all juicy and red.

When I think of love I see red and sky blue
But really Mum, the only person
I love is
      You!

Nicole Stephenson (10)
Wyvil Primary School

Spain

I went to Spain
It was full of rain.
I thought there'd be a hurricane.
Then the sunshine shone bright
Thank God I can fly my kite.
I wanted a tropical fruit
And I saw my cousin dressed in a suit
He looked so cute.

Tasharn Simms (9)
Wyvil Primary School

Happiness

I think happiness is baby blue,
But another thing about happiness
Is it is like hearing joyful singing.
It tastes like bubble gum and mint flavoured ice cream
Mixed together.

Happiness smells like the sweet smell of roses' pollen.
Happiness is like seeing one thousand smiley faces.
Happiness is just another word for feeling joyful.
What does happiness really remind me of?

The joy and love from my family.

Asia Vassel (9)
Wyvil Primary School

Fun

It sounds like joyfulness.
The colours of it are
Baby blue and lilac.
It tastes like strawberries dipped in strawberry sauce.
It smells like Gucci perfume.
It looks like a smiling face.
It feels like a golden sunny day.
It reminds me of a cute
Chubby
		Baby smile!

Rianna Stroude (9) & Suzie Alves (10)
Wyvil Primary School

In The Playground

B ullies pick on children
U nhappy children not knowing who to turn to
L ovely enjoyment they get from bullying
L ovely enjoyment they get from you crying
Y ou must stand up for yourself and be counted
I diots are bullies and get on your nerves
N ever listen to them or you will start to believe what they say
G iving in is not the way, tell a teacher or they will have to pay.

I f in retaliation you hurt them then tell the teacher immediately
S o don't stand back, fight for your rights.

W himpering makes them laugh
R oar with laughter is what they do so don't let them tease you
O h, no, don't let them push you down
N ever be upset by what they say to you
G et up, stand up and be counted.

H airy baboons they are
O uch, words can hurt but a good heart can heal
W ords are very strong weapons.

C lever in teasing but not clever in academics
A rticulate - not their strongest subject
N ever give up on the good things.

W himpering makes them laugh
E ngrossed with bullying.

S ticks and stones may break my bones but words will never hurt me.
T ry to avoid them at all cost
O h, no don't let them push you down
P ractice boxing clever.

I diots are bullies and get on your nerves
T try to avoid them at all costs.

Bullying is wrong. How can we stop it?

Yasmine Gittens-Sextius (9)
Wyvil Primary School

Football Prodigy

I want to be a footballer
And run around the field
Then when they tackle me so hard
I'll block them with my shield.

Then when I go home every day
I will play again in May
I'll score so many goals
And even when I grow up
I'll like to meet Paul Scholes
I'll try and be the best
I'll always have a rest
When I go training
It's always raining.

Deji Adegboyega (8)
Wyvil Primary School

Fun

When I think of fun, I think of the colour baby blue.
I look to the sky, see a robin flying high.
To the Heavens and think of fun.
When I listen, what do I hear?
I hear children laughing and enjoying themselves.
If I was to eat fun it would taste like a bite of pleasure.
When I breathe in I am having fun.
I can always smell the sweet fresh air.
If I was to touch fun it would feel smooth as laminated paper.
Fun reminds me of a wonderful dream.

Natasha Oviri (10)
Wyvil Primary School

Happiness

Happiness is like the colour yellow
It tastes like a sour mango
It's like the game Jenga
Very fun and joyful.
It reminds me of a rainbow
Which comes up in the sky.
It smells like the drink Tango,
Wonderful.
It looks like the church bells ringing
And when your doorbell's dinging.
It sounds like when you're on a boat
Or a policeman's car siren, very loud.
It feels like a bird's feather so smooth and soft.

Happiness is how you should feel every day.

Jermaine Elor (9)
Wyvil Primary School

Life

Waking up in the morning warm as a breeze
Looking at the sky, feeling so pleased.
Another day ahead of us,
Another day so great,
But little do we know what we await.
Seeing children laugh and run
I know this is the life of fun.
Boys and girls getting older
Life getting colder,
Feeling this way from having the world on your shoulders.

Rasak Obanigba (10)
Wyvil Primary School

Extraordinary Teacher

I want to be a good teacher
And teach children to spell
To read and write and how to draw
And teach them not to yell

I'll scream and shout until they learn
And try not to be rude
I'll make sure, I'll look at their books
And change their attitude

The children are very clever
The school is nice and wide
It's colourful and beautiful
And I am on their side.

Qurratuaina Awangkechik (8)
Wyvil Primary School

What I Want To Be

I want to be a good doctor
I'll try to be so keen
I'll give so many injections
I'll try not to be mean.

There'll be so many patients for me
I'll work every day
Except all the resting Sundays
Or then they'll have to pay.

I'll work for the sick and others
I'll try to be the best.
I'll perform so many operations
And then it will be my rest.

Marcio Andrade (9)
Wyvil Primary School

Young Writers - Playground Poets London